S0-AXN-125

CYRUS McCORMICK
and the Mechanical Reaper

CYRUS McCORMICK
and the Mechanical Reaper

Lisa J. Aldrich

**MORGAN
REYNOLDS**
Publishing, Inc.

620 South Elm Street, Suite 223
Greensboro, North Carolina 27406
http://www.morganreynolds.com

ORLAND PARK PUBLIC LIBRARY

CYRUS MCCORMICK AND THE MECHANICAL REAPER

Illustrations courtesy of the Wisconsin State Historical Society.

Library of Congress Cataloging-in-Publication Data

Aldrich, Lisa J., 1952-
  Cyrus McCormick and the mechanical reaper / Lisa J. Aldrich.— 1st ed.

    p. cm.
Summary: Profiles Cyrus Hall McCormick, whose hatred of farm work led
him to invent a machine which made it much quicker and easier to harvest
wheat, and which turned him into a multi-millionaire businessman.
Includes bibliographical references and index.
  ISBN 1-883846-91-9 (lib. bdg.)
  1. McCormick, Cyrus Hall, 1809-1884—Juvenile literature. 2.
Inventors—United States—Biography—Juvenile literature. 3.   Harvesting
machinery—United States—History—Juvenile literature. [1. McCormick,
Cyrus Hall, 1809-1884. 2. Inventors. 3. Harvesting machinery—History.]
I. Title.
  HD9486.U4 M32 2002
  681.763'092—dc21

                          2002002015

Printed in the United States of America
First Edition

With love, appreciation, and great admiration
to my father, Harold O. Bjornstad,
a life-long farmer, and an inventor in his own right;
and in loving memory
of my mother, Beatrice M. Bjornstad,
whose passion for books and writing lives on.

Contents

Cyrus McCormick, 1867

Chapter One

The Valley of Virginia

Cyrus McCormick hated farm work. After he became a wealthy businessman and lived in a Chicago mansion far away from the fields of Virginia where he had spent his youth, he wrote about working in the fields as a boy. He remembered his clothes soaked with sweat, throat parched, shoulders aching from doing a man's work reaping the tall, ripe wheat. Swinging the grain cradle against the wheat was backbreaking and slow. He learned to harvest wheat by watching his father rhythmically swing the cradle as Cyrus's younger brothers, William and Leander, walked behind picking up the stalks of wheat and tying them into bundles. Cyrus thought, standing under the blazing Virginia sun, that surely there must be a way to use horses to harvest wheat.

Cyrus loved tinkering with tools in his father's little, log blacksmith shop. His father was quite an inventor and had already produced several farm tools. Cyrus knew his father was trying to build a mechanical reaper to harvest grain, but so far it had been a disappointment. He just had not been able to make it work.

Young Cyrus McCormick resolved to make a better mechanical reaper and single-mindedly set himself to the task.

Cyrus Hall McCormick was born on his father's farm on February 15, 1809, the first child of Robert and Mary Ann, or "Polly," McCormick. The McCormicks' farm, Walnut Grove, was located on thirty-two acres at the northern edge of Rockbridge County, Virginia, in a long, thin strip of land that was bordered by the Blue Ridge Mountains on the east and the Allegheny Mountains on the west. The nearest town was Staunton, eighteen miles to the north. The Atlantic Ocean was a hundred miles away. The Valley was quiet and its inhabitants worked hard to earn a living.

Robert McCormick was no exception. In the days of his greatest prosperity, he owned four farms totaling twelve hundred acres. He had nine slaves and eighteen horses. But he did much more than plant and harvest crops. He owned two grist mills, two sawmills, a smelting furnace, a distillery, and a blacksmith shop. He also possessed an unusual degree of skill in mechanics. His own father was a weaver, and Robert thus became familiar with machinery at a very young age.

The McCormicks lived in this house on Walnut Grove, the family farm located in the Valley of Virginia.

Robert hammered iron and shaped wood in his black-smith shop with his sons. He invented new types of farm machinery—a hemp brake, a clover huller, a bellows, and a threshing machine. The blacksmith shop was only about twenty-four feet square. It had an uneven floor and a heavy door that hung by homemade nails on homemade hinges. On each side of the chimney was a forge, so that two men could work hot metal at the same time. In later years, Cyrus wrote, "My father was both mechanical and inventive, and could and did at that time, use the tools of his shops in making any piece of machinery he wanted. He invented, made and patented several more or less valuable agricultural implements . . . but most of his inventions dropped into disuse after the lapse of some years."

Cyrus's mother, Polly, was the daughter of a Virginia farmer named Patrick Hall. Mr. Hall had great strength of character, which Polly inherited from him. She was impulsive, highly imaginative, and spoke her mind freely. She was intelligent and very ambitious. She had a strong work ethic and did not allow her children to be idle. If the children were dressed before breakfast, they did not relax and wait to eat. They went outside to chop wood or weed the garden.

The McCormicks were of Scotch-Irish descent. Their ancestors possessed unyielding tenacity and an unconquerable spirit. They were deeply religious people, subscribing to the beliefs of John Knox, who founded the Presbyterian Church in Scotland in the mid-sixteenth century. The Presbyterians were persecuted by the government for their beliefs. They fought mightily and valiantly for their religious freedom, and many of them eventually emigrated from the British Isles to America. By 1776 there were about three hundred thousand Scotch-Irish in the land that would, in 1788, become the United States of America.

During the week, Cyrus and his siblings were instructed each day in Scripture and Catechism, thus receiving a firm ethical foundation, which directed Cyrus's dealings with people for the rest of his life. The McCormick home was filled with hymns, and Cyrus led

Cyrus's mother, Polly, insisted that her children perform housework and chores and attend the local Presbyterian Church.

the congregational singing of the nearby New Providence Church for several years. His voice rose above the congregation as they sang his favorite hymn:

Oh Thou in whose presence my soul takes delight,
On whom in affliction I call,
My comfort by day, and my song in the night,
My hope, my salvation, my all.

Cyrus was deeply moved by music. He especially loved to hear performances by Ole Bull, a Norwegian violinist and composer, and Jenny Lind, a Swedish soprano. He loved to play his own violin and many evenings would go off by himself to play the instrument, enjoying his solitude and the time for reflection.

Food was abundant in the Valley of Virginia, but its inhabitants ate poorly balanced diets. Because of this, as well as a lack of information about sanitation and quarantine, diseases such as yellow fever spread wildly through the Valley of Virginia and took many lives, including those of Polly's parents and brother. Cyrus's first memory of his boyhood was contracting this serious illness at the age of five.

Doctors in those days treated many illnesses by "bleeding," or removing large amounts of blood from the patient. Many people died as a result of this "cure." Cyrus's doctor, who had treated many people during the epidemic, felt exhausted and feared for the lives of his own family by the time Cyrus fell ill. He left the McCormick home, giving a lancet to Robert McCormick with instructions to "bleed" Cyrus. Robert believed that this treatment led only to death, and he decided to try another remedy. He saved little Cyrus by immersing him frequently in hot baths containing bitter herbs and whiskey, and feeding him large amounts of hot tea. Sadly, after saving Cyrus, sixteen-year-old Robert and thirteen-year-old Susan died of dysentery one day apart.

Young Cyrus did not make friends easily, and he spent much of his time alone. He was quiet and re-served, and many in the community criticized him for being aloof. The men in the community around Walnut Grove used foul language, and drank and smoked heavily. Even so, Cyrus decided at a young age that he would not drink alcohol, use tobacco, or swear. His strength of will and self-control enabled him to main-tain this decision throughout his life.

Cyrus was an excellent horseman and was consid-ered to be the best rider in the Valley. He often rode his horse eighteen miles to Lexington or Staunton. There he watched the mail arrive and listened to stagecoach travelers tell their tales of places they had been. Wagon trains carrying immigrants to new homes, groups of slaves chained together and led along to new cotton fields in the Southwest, and huge groups of hogs going north from Kentucky for butchering every autumn were familiar sights.

Young Cyrus was adept at using a gun, but he was teased because he preferred not to join with other boys his age in hunting the abundant bear, deer, fox, and wild turkey of the Valley.

Cyrus paid close attention to the style of his clothing. At the farm, he wore homespun clothes and was often barefoot, but he attended church wearing a broadcloth coat and beaver hat. Many neighbors gossiped about him and criticized him, thinking he was conceited. He became all the more noticeable because, even though Robert and Polly McCormick were each five feet eight inches tall, Cyrus grew in adolescence to six feet two inches and weighed two hundred pounds. He had small hands and feet, but his physique was muscular—he had massive shoulders—and with his wavy, dark brown hair and large dark eyes, he presented an imposing figure.

Cyrus attended the Old Field School not far from his father's farm. One of the family's slaves, Joe Anderson, often walked Cyrus to school to keep him company. The school was made of logs, with part of one of the upper logs cut out to provide a window.

Cyrus sat on a slab bench and studied from various books: *Murray's Grammar*, *Dilworth's Arithmetic*, *Webster's Spelling Book*, *Adams' Geography*, the *New York Primer*, *Titler's History*, *Mrs. D's Philosophy*, the Shorter Catechism, and the Bible. Cyrus and other students also received drawing lessons, using goose quill

Robert McCormick passed on his love for inventing new tools and other farm implements to his son Cyrus.

pens that they dipped in homemade ink. At recess, he played corner-ball and hopscotch with the thirty other students in the school.

Cyrus was a good student and was unusually adept in grammar. He placed great emphasis on correct spelling and punctuation and, in later years, counseled his brother Leander, "You should carry a dictionary, as I do." Even in Cyrus's letters to his family, his sentences were carefully formed and contained no misspelled words.

At fifteen, Cyrus brought to school a very elaborate map of the world, showing both the eastern and the western hemispheres. He had drawn the map in ink on paper and then pasted the paper on a piece of linen fabric. The map hung on two varnished rollers. His teacher was astonished at the depth of his creativity. "That boy is beyond me," she said.

When Cyrus was not in school, he was working very hard on his father's farm, and not liking it much at all.

Chapter Two

Building a Dream

For thousands of years, farmers all over the world harvested grain by hand, using either a sickle, a scythe, or grain cradle. The sickle was invented first and was used by the ancient Egyptians and Babylonians. Broad and heavy, the sickle was a curved, saw-toothed knife set in a wooden handle. The farmer bent down and, holding a few stalks of grain together in one hand, swung the sickle close to the ground and cut the grain. He then lay the handful of stalks on the stubble (the part of the stalks left in the ground after the grain is cut) and repeated the process, hour after hour, from sunrise to sunset. If one man worked all day, he might reap two acres using a sickle.

One or two people, called binders, walked behind the farmer and tied several handfuls of grain into sheaves, using straw for a cord. Others, called shockers or stookers, followed the binders, gathering ten to fifteen sheaves into a "shock" and standing them upright on the ground. Another sheaf was then laid on top of the shock to protect the tender grain from moisture. A woman or boy usually came along with a large rake to clear the stubble of any loose straw and carry it to the binders.

The scythe, invented in Europe by Joseph Jenks in 1655 "for the more speedy cutting of grasse," was more effective than the sickle. It consisted of a long curved blade on a bent wooden stock. On the stock was a handle, and the scytheman used both hands to swing the implement. An experienced scytheman could cut a seven- to eight-foot swath of upright grain from ten to fifteen inches in depth at each stroke. Two or three others assisted him in the binding and shocking. Using a scythe, a farmer could reap no more than three acres in a day.

A Scotsman later attached a device called a cradle to the scythe, and the resulting tool was called a cradle-scythe, or grain cradle. The cradle consisted of three or more narrow, parallel strips of wood, shorter than the scythe blade but curving in a similar manner. It was fastened together with small, wooden crosspieces. The cradle was useful for laying the grain straight in the swath that was made when the grain was cut.

Harvesting was a slow, laborious, and often physically painful process, no matter which method was used. Harvest season is short, generally lasting from four to ten days, and ripe grain decays quickly if it is

Attaching a cradle to the scythe made it easier to collect the grain as it was cut.

not promptly harvested. Each year the farmers in the Valley of Virginia raced against time to harvest as much as possible. If the weather became unfavorable and it began to rain or hail, the entire crop was often lost.

Manual harvesting also severely restricted the size of farms. Farmers planted only the amount of grain that could reasonably be harvested. The bigger the farm, the more laborers were required to harvest the grain.

Laborers did not work for free; seventy-five cents or a dollar was the usual daily wage for an able-bodied man. If the farmer paid more to the laborers than he could sell his crop for, he lost money. Also, laborers were in great demand and often in short supply, and many years the farmer could not find enough men to help with harvest. Without enough manpower, much of the crop often went to waste, and the farmer then turned his pigs into the field to feast on the grain before it rotted completely. Cyrus McCormick figured that if a machine could do the work of a man, the number of laborers needed would be sharply reduced, thus saving the farmer money. The farmer would also be able to harvest more grain in a shorter period of time, enabling him to plant and harvest more acres.

Cyrus's father had tried to invent such a machine but had failed. He devised a mechanical reaper that was pushed through the field from behind by two horses. But the grain only tangled and bunched around the blades, and the reaper became the joke of the neighborhood. After several failed attempts, Robert gave up trying to make a reaper.

Cyrus McCormick was determined to carry on his father's work. In 1831, at the age of twenty-two, Cyrus improved on his father's design for a mechanical reaper. Cyrus's design was influenced by his life as a farmer who had experienced everything that could go wrong during a harvest. He knew that wheat did not always stand tall and straight at harvest time, but often lay tangled on the ground. He knew what a rain storm or high winds could do to grain. An editor of the *Farmer's Register* would later write: "An insurmountable difficulty will sometimes be found to the use of reaping machines in the state of the growing crops, which may be twisted and laid flat in every possible direction. A whole crop may be ravelled and beaten down by high winds and heavy rains in a single day."

Cyrus's reaper would differ from his father's in several important ways. For one thing, instead of being *pushed* through the grain, his reaper would be *pulled* through the grain. It would also have a divider, which would separate the grain that was to be cut from the grain that was left standing. The blade, too, would be changed. In order to cut the separated grain and not miss any of it, the blade needed to cut front to back as well as sideways. McCormick thus gave birth to the idea of the "reciprocating blade," which became the major feature of the reaper.

Another problem McCormick faced was how to support the grain while it was being cut to keep the blade from flattening it to the ground. McCormick devised "guard fingers," a row of deep teeth, much like a comb, on the edge of the blade. The teeth caught the grain, holding it in position to be cut.

McCormick then needed to figure out a way to lift up and straighten the grain that had fallen once it was cut. He made a large revolving reel that swept up the grain, and a platform that caught the grain as it fell. A man who walked alongside the reaper raked the grain off the platform.

By July 1831, McCormick had labored for six weeks

to construct a reaper that worked. Harvest was almost over, but Cyrus had convinced his father to leave one patch of grain standing so that he might try out his reaper. His parents, sisters, and brothers watched as he drove the reaper against the ripened grain. The reel revolved and swept the grain downward toward the knife, the blade moved back and forth, and the grain was cut. It fell upon the platform from where it was raked off by a young man named John Cash. The reel and the divider performed poorly, but nevertheless, the reaper worked.

Excited by the prospect of selling his reaper to other farmers, Cyrus worked the next few days to improve the reel and the divider before he decided the reaper was ready for a public demonstration. He arranged for an exhibition to take place in the nearby town of Steeles Tavern, Virginia. There, using two horses, McCormick cut six acres of oats in an afternoon. The reaper had done the work of six laborers with scythes or twenty-four with sickles.

The following year, 1832, twenty-three-year-old McCormick put on an even larger exhibition in the little village of Lexington, Virginia, eighteen miles south of Walnut Grove. One hundred people attended, including several local political leaders, farmers, professors, laborers, and a group of slaves.

None of the onlookers had seen a reaping machine before, and at first it looked as though the field demonstration was going to be a dismal failure. The field, owned by a man named John Ruff, was hilly, uneven, and full of stones, and the reaper performed poorly on the rough terrain. It jolted and slid so violently that Mr. Ruff is said to have cried: "Here! This won't do! Stop your horses! You are rattling the heads off my wheat."

McCormick was devastated. Several farm laborers who were watching began jeering loudly at him. They were happy that the reaper did not work, for they saw it as competition for their labor. They performed difficult, back-breaking work, but they viewed the reaper the same way the stagecoach drivers would view the railroads, the telegraph operators would view the telephone, or the hackney drivers would view the first automobiles. They feared that the new inventions would put them out of work.

Then a man named William Taylor offered his wheat field as a demonstration site. McCormick had another chance to prove that the reaper worked. Taylor's field was fairly level, and McCormick harvested six acres of wheat. This was no more than he had done the year before, but this time he demonstrated the reaper before a crowd of skeptical strangers.

After this success, the reaper was taken to Lexington and placed in the courthouse square, where it was meticulously studied by Professor Bradshaw of the Lexington Female Academy. After a time, the Professor exclaimed, "This machine is worth a hundred thousand dollars!" McCormick was deeply gratified and encouraged. But nothing meant more to him than the words of his father on that occasion, "It makes me feel proud to have a son do what I could not do."

As impressed as they were, none of the one hundred people who witnessed the demonstration in the town of Lexington purchased a reaper. The world in McCormick's day, and especially the Valley of Virginia, where life moved slowly, was not a place eager to accept new findings in science or new inventions in industry. People were suspicious of progress and were even superstitious. Adherence to tradition was seen as a virtue. For many hundreds of years, farmers had plowed their fields with wooden plows, for they believed that an iron plow, while much sturdier and longer-lasting, would poison the soil. It would not be easy to convince farmers to change age-old ways of doing things.

McCormick did not know it at the time, but he was not the first to build a reaper that cut grain. Twenty-three people in Europe, and the same number in America, had manufactured reapers, but all their machines were inefficient. None of these inventors had achieved what McCormick had. His design was far superior, and it is doubtful that any of the forty-six other reapers could have been improved into a workable machine.

It was a tribute to McCormick's skill and inventiveness that rivals who built reapers in later years copied his design—though McCormick never saw it that way.

Perhaps McCormick found success with his reaper because he was the only inventor who was actually a farmer. The others were clergymen, sailors, schoolteachers, even an actor. None of them had his years of experience working a harvest. Maybe McCormick's dislike of farming during his youth motivated him to work harder to develop a machine to free him from the work. For whatever reasons, the other reapers might work in ideal conditions, on perfectly straight grain on a perfectly level field in perfect weather, but they would fail miserably when faced with actual harvest conditions. By dealing with these problems, Cyrus had built the world's first practical mechanical reaper.

Chapter Three

War of the Reapers

Cyrus did not want to be a farmer. One summer day in 1832, McCormick was riding home on horseback. His horse stopped in the middle of a stream to drink. As McCormick looked out upon the nearby fields of grain shimmering in the sunlight, an awe-inspiring thought came to him, "Perhaps I may make a million dollars from this reaper." Years later in a letter, he wrote, "This thought was so enormous that it seemed like a dream— like dwelling in the clouds—so remote, so unattainable, so exalted, so visionary."

McCormick decided to take his reaper and create a business. Thus far, the only people who knew of his reaper lived in his little valley. How was he to let the world know that his reapers would provide them a better way to harvest? How could he convince others to buy them?

He was not going to be content to merely build a few

reapers in his father's blacksmith shop and sell them one by one. He wanted to be rich, and that meant selling many more reapers than he could build himself. He decided to accomplish his goal by building a business to manufacture and sell reapers.

McCormick had a lot of motivation, creativity, and energy. What he did not have was money. He would have to buy materials to make his reapers and would need even more money to market and advertise the machine. The idea of advertising his reaper was radical and brilliant. Advertising was largely unheard of at the time, and of the 850 newspapers published in the United States in 1832, not one of them had yet mentioned his reaper.

McCormick set out to get publicity. The first printed notice of the reaper appeared in the *Lexington Union* on September 14, 1833. The article, entitled "Important Invention," included testimonials from three farmers who, although they did not use the reaper themselves, had seen it at work. No sales resulted from this one article, but this did not deter McCormick. He was convinced that advertising would eventually work.

This persistence, even stubbornness, was a dominant characteristic of McCormick. He was always sure he was right and was not easily diverted by criticism or doubt. This competitive single-mindedness also made him antagonistic toward anyone he thought was treating him unfairly or was stealing his ideas. There is an old adage that says "Imitation is the sincerest form of flattery." To McCormick, however, imitation was a threat to his dignity and livelihood. He was determined to fight for what he believed was his. One of the first and best examples of McCormick's nature was the competition he shared with another reaper manufacturer named Obed Hussey. Their ongoing feud over whose machine was better became known as the "War of the Reapers."

McCormick soon discovered that he had a fierce rival in the reaper business. Obed Hussey was born in Maine to Quaker parents in 1792 and later moved to Nantucket, Massachusetts. He set out to become a sailor to "sail about a little and see the watery part of the world." He rowed skiffs after whales in the Pacific Ocean and somewhere along the way lost an arm and his left eye. Those losses may be why he left the sea and began to dabble in mechanics. Those who knew him described him as caring and sensitive and not prone to glory-seeking. McCormick characteristically saw him as a tenacious, unyielding, stubborn enemy who would not leave him alone.

In 1832, Hussey was living on a farm near Cincinnati, Ohio, that was owned by Judge A. Foster. Hussey had invented a machine for stamping out pins and fish hooks, and another that made candles. A friend asked him why he did not construct a machine to reap grain. Whoever invented one, his friend added, would surely make a fortune.

Although he knew little about farming, Hussey constructed a reaper that performed so well he took it to the Hamilton County Agricultural Society Fair at Carthage, Ohio, on July 2, 1833. The demonstration was such a success that a man named Jarvis Reynolds loaned Hussey enough money to begin manufacturing his reaper. In December 1833, Hussey was granted a patent and began manufacturing in Cincinnati. McCormick had not yet applied for a patent, but when he read about Hussey's patent and saw a woodcut of Hussey's reaper in *Mechanics' Magazine* in April 1834, he became enraged. He wrote a letter to the editor of the magazine on May 20, 1834:

> Dear Sir:
> Having seen in the April number of your Mechanics' Magazine a cut and description of a reaping machine, said to have been invented by Mr. Obed Hussey, of Ohio, last summer, I would ask the favor of you to inform Mr. Hussey, and the public, through your columns, that the principle, viz., cutting grain by the means of a toothed instrument, receiving a rotary motion from a crank, with the iron teeth projecting before the edge of the cutter for the purpose of preventing the grain from partaking of its motion, is a part of the principle of my machine, and was invented by me, and operated on wheat and oats in July, 1831. This can be attested to the entire satisfaction of the public and Mr. Hussey, as it was wit-

nessed by many persons; consequently, I would warn
all persons against the use of the aforesaid principle,
as I regard and treat the use of it, in any way, as an
infringement of my right.

Hussey made no reply to McCormick's letter. He had
already sold a few reapers, though none in or near
Virginia. He had found another manufacturer to produce reapers for him in New York, and he now had
customers in New York, Ohio, and Maryland.

Because he was not a farmer, Hussey did not know of
the challenges of harvest. He first designed his machine and, as he learned more about farming, he tried to
adapt it to the field.

Hussey's machine was less complicated than
McCormick's. It had no reel and worked more like a
mower than a reaper. The platform the grain fell on after
it was cut was on the right of the machine, rather than
on the back. It was raked from the platform onto the
ground directly behind the machine and required five
to seven workers to remove the cut grain as fast as
possible so that the reaper and the horses would not
trample it on the next round. Hussey's reaper was much
heavier, requiring three or four horses to pull, instead
of two.

McCormick had not yet sold any reapers when he
paid thirty dollars to the U.S. Treasury and, on June 21,
1834, was issued a patent on his invention. He was the

Obed Hussey was one of McCormick's first, and most tenacious, rivals in the mechanical reaper business.

forty-seventh person to obtain a reaper patent. The patent was good for fourteen years and granted him "the full and exclusive right and liberty of making, constructing, using and vending to others to be used, the said improvement."

Although he had a patent, McCormick did not have a manufacturing business. He decided to concentrate on farming the 473 acres of land that his father had recently given him, in hopes of earning enough to begin his reaper manufacturing business. There was a small log house on the land that he lived in with two elderly slaves. McCormick did not share his mother's staunch pro-slavery attitudes, nor was he an abolitionist. He supported the gradual emancipation of the slaves and felt that abolitionists, by forcing the issue before the time was right, were responsible for the increasing belligerence of the South's pro-slavery arguments. He also said that if the federal government freed the slaves, slaveowners ought to be compensated.

McCormick worked his farm for a year before realizing that he would never raise enough money from farming to be able to begin manufacturing reapers. He needed another way to earn money. Near his farm was a large deposit of iron ore. In later years, he wrote: "In 1836, full of enterprise and not satisfied to rest on my oars nor on my inventions, an opportunity was presented to me to engage in the iron business . . . The dignity and position of an iron-master was somewhat enviable."

McCormick and his father became business partners in 1836 and began building reapers in their workshop at Walnut Grove.

At the time, iron cost fifty dollars a ton—two and one half cents per pound. Iron was the most expensive material used in making McCormick's reaper. A successful iron business would provide Cyrus with both capital and the raw material he needed to build reapers.

McCormick persuaded his father to enter the business with him. The two went into partnership with Daniel Matthews, an experienced ironworker, on September 12, 1836. First they built a furnace to smelt the iron, and by 1837, they were making iron.

They planned for Matthews to manage the operation, but he soon proved to be a disappointment. McCormick fired him in the fall of 1837, and Matthews promptly filed a lawsuit arguing that he was a partner and could not be fired. The case dragged on in court for five years—eventually McCormick won.

At the time of Matthew's firing, John S. Black, a local bachelor who was said to be very wealthy, joined the partnership. For two years the business flourished. Then, in 1839, the price of iron fell. That same year McCormick gave another public exhibition of the reaper on the farm of Joshua Smith, near the town of Staunton. He cut two acres of wheat in one hour. Again, the on-lookers were impressed, but no one bought a reaper. Although the reaper did the work of ten men, there was a surplus of human labor at the time and a shortage of hard cash. It was easier, and maybe wiser, to keep doing things the old way.

Because of the slowdown in the iron business in 1839, McCormick's relationship with Black began to deteriorate. The firm owed money to many creditors, and Black refused to help with the bills. He claimed that he had already put more than his share of money into the business. McCormick ended the partnership and sued Black. (The case against Black was not settled until 1846, when McCormick finally accepted a check for five hundred dollars.)

In the meantime, McCormick could not pay his creditors without Black's help. He had to give up his farm and other property, but he did not give up his reaper patent—although no one would have taken it if he had been willing to part with it. Without a thriving business behind it, the patent was worthless. Instead of being a millionaire, he was eight years older than when he built his first reaper, and penniless.

Even though he had no money, McCormick was more determined than ever to sell his reaper. He began to do what he thought was impossible before: manufacturing reapers with no start-up money. His father and brothers joined him, and the little log blacksmith shop on his father's farm became their factory. Cyrus secured the raw materials and arranged for their transportation over canals.

The following year, Obed Hussey moved his headquarters to Maryland. He sold a few machines, but business was not good. He demonstrated his machine in farmers' fields, contacted several newspapers, and advertised. But he made the mistake of over-promising—he made his reaper sound so good that it turned out to be a disappointment when the farmers actually saw it work. He claimed they would reap twenty acres in a day, which they almost never did. In 1840, Hussey bragged: "I consider myself alone successful . . . Every previous attempt has totally failed and gone into oblivion." The farmers grew tired of Hussey's boasting and his claims that rarely came true. His sales continued to drop, and his reputation was damaged.

One day in 1840, a rough-looking stranger on horseback approached the McCormick farm. He had attended the Staunton exhibition the year before and was impressed with the reaper demonstration. Though he could not afford to buy a reaper at the time, he had made up his mind that he was going to save up fifty dollars so he could purchase one. His name was Abraham Smith, and he was Cyrus McCormick's first customer.

Two weeks later, two more strangers arrived at the McCormick farm. They had ridden forty miles through the Blue Ridge Mountains. Neither had ever seen a reaper, but they had heard of it. Both farmers ordered machines, but McCormick would accept an order for only one of them. One of the farmers planned to use his to harvest wet grain, and McCormick was not satisfied with the way the reaper performed in wet grain. If the grain was not dry, it was likely to get stuck in the blade. McCormick, although poor and desperate to build his business, knew that a farmer complaining that the reaper did not perform as advertised would be much more damaging than would the proceeds from a single sale. He was more interested in making and selling a satisfactory product than in making quick money. After nine years, he had sold two reapers.

Challenged by the lost sale, Cyrus focused on solving the problem of cutting wet grain. After making the edge of the reaper's blade even more serrated than it had been, the reaper cut wet grain nearly as easily as dry grain. Because he was working on the reaper blade to solve the wet grain problem in 1841, he sold no reapers that year.

William Massie, a long-time neighbor, came to believe in McCormick's work and lent him money during times of financial urgency. On April 3, 1841, McCormick wrote to Massie: "I am frank to say that I scarcely know how we would have got along through these difficult times but for your assistance—times that have brought low many of the most noble, the adventurous spirits of the land." By July 1846, McCormick had fully repaid Massie for every dollar he borrowed from him.

By 1842, he had a much-improved reaper and decided to try pitching a sale. He set the price for the reaper at one hundred dollars and began to actively sell his machine by talking to individual farmers. The first purchaser, Abraham Smith, had given him a glowing written testimonial, and McCormick became a salesman. He rode on horseback over mountain roads to spread the word about his reaper.

McCormick published an advertisement in a newspaper stating that he "intend[ed] to devote his attention exclusively to introducing his machines in different parts of the country . . . guaranteeing their performance in every respect; and if they perform as warranted to do, it will be seen, as stated also by others, that they will pay for themselves in one year's use . . . and if so, what tolerable farmer [could] hesitate to purchase?"

Hussey read the advertisements and viewed them as a challenge. In March 1843, he responded in a letter to the *Richmond Southern Planter*:

It shall be my endeavor to meet the machine in the field in the next harvest. I think it but justice to give this public notice that the parties concerned may not be taken unawares, but have the opportunity to prepare themselves for such a contest, that no advantage may be taken. Those gentlemen who have become prudently cautious, by being often deceived by humbugs, will then have an opportunity to judge for themselves.

McCormick and Hussey had demonstrated their machines in non-competitive field trials but had never met face to face on a field. In early June 1843, McCormick delighted a crowd at the Henrico Agricultural and Horticultural Society Fair with a field exhibition. The president of the society bought a McCormick reaper on the spot and several other sales followed that day. McCormick decided to establish a temporary base of operation at the farm of the Reverend Jesse W. Turner, near Richmond. By June 20, Hussey, hearing of McCormick's success and not wanting to be outdone, sent two of his reapers to the editor of the *Southern Planter*. He arrived in Richmond several days later, and the bitterness and ill-will between McCormick and Hussey began immediately.

Reverend Turner had previously been asked by a local farmer, Ambrose Hutchinson, to help him harvest his twenty-five acres of wheat. Turner, being a man who enjoyed competition, approached Hutchinson and suggested that he allow McCormick and Hussey to race their reapers on his farm. Hutchinson agreed, and the contest was set for June 30. The War of the Reapers had found its first battlefield.

On June 24, McCormick published a letter to the *Richmond Enquirer*, challenging Hussey: "I have thought it due to myself, and to those gentlemen who have invested money in my machine, to avail myself of the earliest opportunity of accepting the proposition for a trial of the two machines upon the same ground." McCormick also said that he would let the farmers be the judges, that he would start at sunrise, before the morning dew evaporated, to prove that his reaper would cut damp wheat. He also said he could harvest fifteen acres in a day, using two horses and two operators.

The editor of the *Richmond Enquirer* had prefaced McCormick's letter by saying: "From the following challenge, we may look out for some 'rare fun'—not on the 'battle' but on the 'wheat' field . . . Much good always follows such a struggle for superiority, conducted, as it will be, in the most friendly spirit."

During the week before the June 30 contest, McCormick and Hussey were busy giving field demonstrations around the Richmond area. On June 27, McCormick was on the estate of E.L. Wight, when to his surprise, Hussey showed up. Hussey had been telling the neighborhood that he planned to "give McCormick a go" on the Wight field. A small crowd had gathered, and before the reaping began, a rain shower completely soaked the grain. Hussey's reaper could not cut the wet wheat. McCormick's reaper, which cut the wheat beautifully, was declared the better of the two.

Disgruntled, Hussey took his two reapers to a nearby plantation to prepare for the upcoming contest. He took the bigger and better of his two reapers across a bridge to an island in the James River, where he planned to practice reaping. After Hussey arrived on the island, the bridge was swept away by high water, and he was unable to get his best machine back ashore in time for the June 30 contest.

On the morning of June 30, McCormick arrived in Hutchinson's field as promised and began to reap the grain at dawn. Hussey appeared with his reaper at noon. Thirty or forty watched, judges were appointed, and the contest began. Even though he took two hours off for the noon meal, McCormick harvested seventeen acres of grain that day, while Hussey barely managed two. McCormick was declared the winner.

Hussey argued that the contest was unfair because his best reaper was stuck on the island in the middle of the James River. He told the judges that if he had been able to use the other reaper, he would have beat McCormick.

One of the judges, W.H. Roane, invited McCormick and Hussey to a contest during the following week in his own wheat field at Tree Hill. The two men accepted. The day of the contest, McCormick saw that part of the wheat was tangled and lodged (lying down). He refused to try his reaper on the damaged wheat, but cut fourteen acres in other parts of the field. Hussey confidently drove his heavy reaper onto the lodged wheat and immediately broke the sickle and rake. Even so, this time Roane believed that Hussey's reaper was superior, and ordered one from him for the next harvest season.

For the next two years, the War of the Reapers continued in letters printed in the *Southern Planter*. After printing Hussey's most recent letter, the editor, Charles T. Botts, announced in the March 1845, issue: "This thing must end somewhere, and this is the last of it. If these gentlemen desire to continue this controversy they must seek some other arena . . . Our subscribers . . . are worn out and sick of the whole matter."

In spite of Botts's insistence that McCormick and Hussey end their battle in his newspaper, McCormick answered Hussey's letter. Botts refused to publish it, stating that the argument between them had "degenerated into a personal matter." If any readers were still interested in McCormick's reply to Hussey, he said they could come to the newspaper office and read it there.

Overall, McCormick had won that year's contest. There was no doubt that his reaper was more popular: He sold twenty-nine reapers in 1843, while Hussey sold only two. McCormick was finally experiencing some success.

Chapter Four

Expansion

Walnut Grove was now devoted entirely to the manufacture of the reaper. With the help of his brothers and
father, the business grew, and by 1844, they had sold
fifty reapers at one hundred dollars each. But, as he
became more successful, McCormick ran into obstacles.
Some farmers failed to pay for their machines. Four
machines were held up on canal boats and were not
delivered until after harvest was over. McCormick sent
a man whom he trusted to collect three hundred dollars
from farmers who owed him money, but the man collected it and then ran away with both the money and the
horse McCormick had loaned him. But none of these
setbacks deterred McCormick. He knew he had a product that could change farming forever, and he was determined to let the world know about it.

Several farmers were so impressed with the reaper
they asked McCormick if they could sell them for him,

or become his agents. One was a man named James M. Hite. "My reaper has more than paid for itself in one harvest," Hite said after he had cut a record 175 acres in less than eight days. He paid McCormick $1,333 for the right to sell reapers in eight Virginia counties. Soon Colonel M. Tutwiler agreed to pay twenty-five hundred dollars for the right to sell in southern Virginia. Not long after, Jabez Parker, a manufacturer in Richmond, became an agent in five counties. McCormick signed contracts with the men stating that they would remain his agents until 1848, when the original patent of 1834 would run out. He agreed to pay each agent a "commission," a percentage of sales, on the reapers they sold.

The agents soon discovered that their job had many duties. They had to maintain a sample machine so farmers could see a reaper before they bought one. They traveled throughout their territory to talk to farmers about the reaper—farmers who may not have heard of it yet. After a farmer bought a reaper, the agent was responsible for delivering the machine and for showing the farmer how it worked. He had to keep spare parts on hand and do repairs on the reapers when needed. Agents also had to collect money from the farmers and prepare and send reports to McCormick. They also distributed advertisements throughout their territories.

After witnessing McCormick's success, several other inventors built and tried to sell reapers of their own, but most failed in a short time. Nevertheless, McCormick provided his agents with information on his rivals' reapers so they could offer intelligent comparisons to the farmers.

Even though McCormick improved the reaper every year, there were still complaints from farmers that the agents had to address. The gears on the reaper of 1853 failed and had to be replaced free of charge. Often farmers let reapers in need of repair stand in fields over the winter, right where they broke down, and did not call the agents for repairs until just before the next harvest. Of course by then the farmers needed the repairs immediately, and the agents were especially busy. An expert mechanic who was sent out to the field to help an agent with such repairs wrote, "The machines are in the worst plight imaginable. I have found them outdoors and frozen down just where they last used them."

McCormick urged the agents not to sell a reaper to any farmer to whom they would not lend their own money. To reinforce this lesson, McCormick made the agents wait for the greater part of their commission on each sale until the farmer had paid for his reaper. These rules were often relaxed for immigrant farmers from Germany and Norway because they had a very high reputation for being honest and thrifty. Despite McCormick's cautionary advice to his agents, however, they sometimes still had trouble collecting money.

Overall, McCormick was generous to his customers.

Because farmers did not usually have money to pay for the reapers until after harvest, McCormick decided to extend credit to help them buy his reapers.

He understood that a farmer got paid once a year—after the summer harvest. He extended credit to farmers so that they could receive their new reapers in time for harvest, but not pay for them until afterward. He asked the farmer to pay one-third plus the cost of shipping the reaper up front. The balance was due December 1, along with six percent interest, which accrued from the previous July 1. The local agents were urged to keep strictly to these terms. However, they often departed from them. In reality, agents often agreed to accept as little as one-tenth from the farmers when they delivered their machines, and collected the remaining money—when it was possible to collect it at all—any time within in the next eighteen months.

McCormick used the credit system to help his business grow more rapidly. He obviously lost some money this way, but he had a charitable, open-minded attitude about some losses—which helped him build long-term relationships with his customers. Sometimes, farmers lost their entire crops due to bad weather or grasshopper infestation. When grasshoppers ruined the crops in Webster City, Iowa, many of McCormick's buyers in the area could not meet their financial obligations to him. McCormick traveled to Webster City and shook hands with each of the farmers who owed him money. He then promised them that he would see them through their difficulty and not pressure them for the money they owed. The farmers were so grateful that they eventually paid McCormick every penny, and for years afterward only McCormick reapers were sold in Webster City.

During the years between 1842 and 1844, McCormick reapers began to sell to farmers outside of Virginia. Seven were sold to farmers in the West—two in Tennessee and one each in Wisconsin, Missouri, Iowa, Illinois, and Ohio. Newspaper editors were finally writing and printing advertisements about the "Virginia Reaper," as it was now called. The seven western farmers had seen these advertisements and had placed orders with McCormick.

As more orders came in from western farmers, transportation became a bigger problem. It was difficult and expensive to ship the reapers hundreds of miles away. They had to be carried in wagons to Scottsville, then taken by canal to Richmond, where they were reloaded onto barges and shipped down the James River to the Atlantic Ocean. From there they were shipped around Florida to New Orleans and transferred to a river boat that traveled up the Mississippi and Ohio Rivers to Cincinnati. From Cincinnati they would be moved in various directions to waiting farmers. However, the reapers did not always arrive in time for harvest, and as a result some farmers refused to pay for them.

It became obvious to McCormick that Virginia was not the best place to manufacture reapers that were being sold to farmers on the plains. A friend suggested that McCormick begin manufacturing the reapers in what was then known as the West, the land west of the Appalachian Mountains. The farms there were larger and the land was more level and much less rocky, which made the reaper more productive. Farm labor was also scarce in the less populated West, and farmers in places such as Illinois and Indiana had a hard time finding enough men to work the harvest. Large portions of the crops were often lost because they could not be harvested before the grain spoiled or was destroyed by inclement weather.

The more McCormick thought about his friend's suggestion, the better he liked the idea of establishing a manufacturing center west of the Appalachians. He set off on a three thousand mile journey, with three hundred dollars in his pocket, traveling through Pennsylvania by stagecoach to Lake Ontario, then west through Ohio, Michigan, Illinois, Wisconsin, Iowa, and Missouri.

McCormick was in awe of what he saw on the prairies. The Valley of Virginia was stony, hilly, and full of tree stumps. Here there were vast plains of flat, fertile soil.

As he rode through Illinois, he saw hogs and cattle feeding on great fields of ripe grain for lack of laborers to harvest it. People all over the world were starving, and this grain that could easily feed them was going to waste. The rich soil of Illinois had produced five million bushels of wheat, but it was too much for the sickle and the scythe to cut. Farmers and their wives, children, and hired laborers worked day and night to bring in the crops, but the grain rotted before they could harvest it all.

The West was McCormick's ideal marketplace. He did not believe it would take long to convince the farmers there to buy the reaper. His first task was to overcome the transportation problem. Whereas before he had enlisted agents to sell the machines he manufactured in Virginia, he decided on this trip to sell licenses to several manufacturers in the West who would make the reapers for him. This idea was a forerunner of the modern franchise system. The manufacturers would produce and sell the reapers. McCormick would receive a portion of the sale as payment for using his patent.

McCormick left Walnut Grove again in 1844 and traveled across the country several times between Chicago, Cincinnati, and Brockport, New York, searching for trustworthy and capable manufacturers for his reapers in those areas. The transportation problem was always on his mind. While on his journey West, he wrote to his family from Indiana, "It seems wrong to pay $20 or $25 freight . . . when they [reapers] might be made in the West—considering, too, the greater uncertainty of shipping."

Within months, McCormick had sold manufacturing licenses to Backus, Fitch & Company of Brockport, New York; Seymour, Morgan & Company, also in Brockport; Henry Bear in Missouri; Gray & Warner in Illinois; and A.C. Brown in Cincinnati. If all went according to plan, McCormick's reapers would be used on farms from the Potomac River to the Missouri River within a year.

McCormick enjoyed some success in the harvest of 1846. H.E. Towner of Will County, Illinois, said in July 1846, "I consider it [the McCormick Reaper] to the western country the most important invention of the age, and that it will greatly increase the product of the country, not being able without it to reap so much as can be sown." That same month, the editor of the *Chi-*

cago Daily Journal stated that the McCormick reaper "will cut from 15 to 20 acres per day, which is as decided an advance upon the old method of 'cradling' as the Magnetic Telegraph is on steam. These machines are highly useful in this State, where the harvest is large, while the means of saving it is disproportionally small."

McCormick was encouraged by these testimonials. It seemed that farmers in the West were quick to realize the value of the reaper. McCormick made arrangements with his Illinois manufacturers, C.M. Gray and S.R. Warner, to manufacture one hundred more reapers for the harvest of 1847.

However, there were problems with the harvest of 1846. Manufacturers did not always make reapers that measured up to McCormick's strict standards. Some used inferior raw materials, or hired unskilled workers to build the machines. Several farmers did not get their reapers in time for harvest. Henry Bear built only twenty of the thirty reapers he promised McCormick, and only four of them worked properly. Brown had promised McCormick he would make two hundred, but actually built less than one hundred, and they were all defective. Backus, Fitch & Co. did not build even one. McCormick had hoped to have four hundred reapers working in the West during the harvest of 1846. As it was, he had barely seventy-five. He needed to find a way to better control his licensed manufacturers. The thought of the prairies being filled with inferior reapers and of dissatisfied and angry farmers appalled him.

News from Walnut Grove was not good, either. Although his family had manufactured and sold forty-eight reapers in 1846, public opinion was swinging back in favor of Hussey's reaper. Hussey discovered that the McCormick reapers made by Hite were inferior and easily beaten by his own. Jabez Parker, who had made excellent McCormick reapers, was dead, and Parker's son did not seem to want to carry on the business. McCormick's brother Leander, who was very valuable in the Walnut Grove shop because of his extraordinary mechanical skill, had married in October 1845 and was eager to settle down on a farm of his own.

One event overshadowed all the troubles McCormick faced during the harvest of 1846. His father had been Cyrus's advisor and best friend as the two worked side by side for years to make harvesting easier and more profitable for the farmer. Robert was a dreamer; Cyrus had the motivation and drive to makes dreams a reality. As the years went on, they became more than partners and father and son—they were firm friends.

Robert had always enjoyed good health, but one winter night he rushed out of the house to extinguish a fire in one of the shops. It was bitterly cold, and in his haste to put out the fire, Robert had not put on warm clothing before he went outside. He caught a severe cold, and though he was largely recovered by the time McCormick left for the West, his body was damaged and other illnesses quickly followed. He continued to work until May, when his doctor insisted that he stop. For two months his family lived alternately between hope and despair.

McCormick knew of his father's condition, yet he was so occupied with his reaper business that he did not return to Walnut Grove. The family's pastor, Reverend James Morrison, wrote to McCormick on May 30, 1846:

> You know well that every attention that human kindness can bestow he [Robert] receives. Every member of his kind family takes pleasure in doing everything they can for his comfort . . . He is calm, composed . . . perfectly resigned to the will of God. You well know that he is well instructed in the truths of the Bible . . . I have discovered no fear of death in him . . . God has indeed been very kind to you. Your privileges have been very great. You have had parents such as are equaled by few.

Robert McCormick died on July 4, 1846.

Following his father's death, McCormick experienced profound grief for the first time in his life. He was emotionally numb and felt utterly alone. Late in the summer of 1846, he wrote to his brother William: "I often wonder whether you who have been present throughout the illness and at the death of our *lost* father, could have been and continue to be so deeply affected by it as I have. I should think not, as in all my reflections, it seems but a little while since I saw him and left him well,—and my returning and not again meeting him often shocks me."

In the spring of 1847, McCormick once again traveled west. He had sent his brother Leander to Cincinnati to oversee production at the A.C. Brown plant. William was left alone to build reapers in Walnut Grove. He manufactured thirty-five that year, but all were defective and unable to be sold. William lacked his brother's mechanical talent and did not respond well to the pressure of maintaining the farm.

McCormick was torn. His business had grown to the point that he could not supervise all his manufacturers by himself. Yet many millions of acres of western prairie still lay uncultivated. Finally he came to a conclusion: He must build a large reaper factory in the West. He did not know where exactly. The new railroads were slowly proceeding westward, yet water transportation was still very crucial. He must locate his factory at a spot where grain, transportation facilities—both rail and water—and building materials were all available.

Cleveland, Ohio; Milwaukee, Wisconsin; and St. Louis, Missouri, were all prosperous cities, but none had everything McCormick required to locate his factory. Only one place met all his criteria. Although it was a young city and still small, McCormick decided to build his new reaper factory in Chicago, Illinois.

Chapter Five

Chicago

By appearances, Chicago should have been the last place McCormick would choose to build his factory. In 1847, when McCormick first visited, the city was plagued with mud, dust, floods, and droughts. Inhabited by seventeen thousand people, Chicago's economy was failing, and banks were going out of business. The Chicago River was polluted by the waste dumped from the stockyards that lined its banks. Drinking its water resulted in repeated cholera outbreaks, and smallpox killed hundreds. Street sanitation conditions were no better. As the *Gem of the Prairie* described them: "Many of the populous localities are noisome quagmires, the gutters running with filth at which the very swine turn up their noses in supreme disgust . . . The gutters at the crossings are clogged up, leaving standing pools of an indescribable liquid, there to salute the noses of passers-by."

Most of the houses were rickety, unpainted shacks with no house numbers. There were no paved streets, except for one short block of wooden paving. Chicago had one school, a jail, a theater, a fire engine, and six policemen, but there was no railroad, telegraph, gas, or sewer. The post office, housed in a little shack on Clark Street, had one window and one clerk.

Residents of other cities ridiculed Chicago and called it a mud hole. The harbor was obstructed by a sand bar, and the entire surrounding region, stretching for miles back from Lake Michigan, was a swamp.

McCormick somehow saw beyond the mud and dilapidation of the city. He realized that Chicago, by virtue of its location on Lake Michigan and the Chicago River—and their proximity to the Mississippi River—was the most important link between the eastern United States and the West. Receiving the raw materials he needed to manufacture his reapers would be easy in Chicago. Using ships on the Great Lakes for transportation, he could get his steel from Sheffield, his pig-iron from Scotland and Pittsburgh, and his white ash from Michigan. He could also use the same waterways to ship his reapers both east and west.

Others saw the potential, too, and over the next decade, the population of Chicago boomed. Immigrants from Europe, mostly from Ireland and Germany, poured into the city, overwhelming its already meager infrastructure. Railroads and canals, often funded by government money arranged by powerful Illinois Senator Stephen Douglas, brought even more growth.

McCormick still needed capital, and the best way to get that was to find a partner. In August 1847, Charles M. Gray and Seth Warner, who had been making reapers for McCormick in Chicago, ended their partnership. They still owed McCormick twenty-five hundred dollars in patent fees. McCormick decided to form a partnership with Gray, and did so on August 30, 1847.

On the same day that McCormick and Gray formed their partnership, they also bought three lots situated near a pier on Lake Michigan from William B. Ogden, the most powerful man in Chicago. Born in New York in 1805, he was similar to McCormick in background and personality. Describing his own character, Ogden said he "was born close to a saw mill, was early left an orphan, christened in a mill pond, taught at a log school house, and at fourteen fancied that nothing was impossible, which ever since, and with some success, I have been trying to prove."

When Ogden moved to Chicago, he quickly made a fortune in real estate and served as the city's first mayor. He had built the first beautiful home in the city, promoted the first canal, and was now engaged in building the first railroad from Chicago northwestward to Galena.

McCormick and Gray decided to build a factory on the land they purchased from Ogden. The factory, the

Cyrus McCormick decided to build his new reaper factory in Chicago.

biggest in the city, would be powered by a thirty-horse-power steam engine.

The partnership contract drawn up between McCormick and Gray stated that Gray was responsible for paying for and overseeing the construction of the factory, including the purchase and installation of equipment. He would also supervise the building of the reapers. He would "keep regular and correct accounts subject to Cyrus H. McCormick's inspection at all times," and to furnish McCormick monthly financial statements showing how much money had been spent and how much would be required for running the business. For this work, the company, which they called McCormick & Gray, would pay him one thousand dollars a year.

McCormick and Gray planned to build five hundred reapers for the harvest of 1848. McCormick was to receive a thirty dollar patent fee for each of those reapers, for a total of fifteen thousand dollars. He was also to be paid two dollars a day for the time that he spent away from the factory on company business.

McCormick and Gray were to divide the net profits from the business, and each was to pay half of the cost of manufacturing the reapers. The money that Gray spent on the necessary supplies and machinery would count toward his half of the cost he had to pay.

On August 30, both men agreed to invest two thousand dollars in the company. Before the end of the year,

McCormick was to put in another two thousand dollars, and on January 1, 1848, "and monthly thereafter, to deposit in like manner whatever sum is required to make up his half of the capital required for the business."

The contract did not state that Gray was responsible to pay McCormick the twenty-five hundred dollars that he and Warner owed him at the end of their partnership. McCormick thought that Gray understood that he still had to pay the twenty-five hundred dollars. Gray did not see it that way. This misunderstanding planted the seed of their future problems.

Gray and McCormick began building the factory soon after purchasing the land from Ogden. It would take three years to finish. At the end of 1847, McCormick left for Washington, D.C. His 1834 patent was to expire the next year, and he was determined to renew it for another seven years. (He had also received patents in 1845 and 1847 on improvements he had made to the original 1831 reaper.) The renewal process was very long and involved and kept him away from Chicago for much of the year.

McCormick left Gray in charge of the Chicago operations. The winter of 1847-48 was a bad one and wheat crops did not fare well. Gray anticipated poor profits from the harvest and, in a panic, he went to William B. Ogden and William E. Jones in January 1848, pretending to be in great need of money to carry on the business. He lied, saying that McCormick had failed to furnish his portion of the money. Ogden and Jones promised Gray a loan of seven thousand dollars in exchange for one half of his ownership in the business. Gray did not send McCormick a monthly financial statement, as they had agreed upon.

McCormick was outraged when, in July 1848, he learned what Gray had done. He retorted that Gray's accusation that he had not provided his share of the money was "untrue and false." A series of bitterly contested court cases followed that eventually led all the way to the Supreme Court, where McCormick was awarded thirty thousand dollars.

Despite Gray's belief that the harvest of 1848 would be a poor one, all but thirteen of the five hundred reapers McCormick & Gray manufactured were sold. On October 7, 1848, the *Gem of the Prairie* announced that Cyrus McCormick, William B. Ogden, and William E. Jones had entered into a partnership. The new reaper manufacturing firm was to be called McCormick, Ogden & Co. But this partnership was not destined to last, either.

McCormick and Ogden were too much alike—both were strong and domineering. Each had his own ideas about how the business should be run. McCormick was interested only in the reaper business, whereas Ogden had other interests and did not give his full attention to the factory. They found they could not cooperate with each other. The two men did not quarrel, but on September 10, 1849, McCormick bought out Ogden and Jones for sixty-five thousand dollars.

During the trouble with Gray in 1848, McCormick faced another battle in Washington, D.C., over the renewal of his patent. Many other businessmen were now interested in manufacturing reapers modeled after McCormick's machines. According to U.S. Patent Law, McCormick could not sue a reaper manufacturer who built a reaper with either a reel, a divider, or a platform, because he did not invent any one of these by itself. But if the manufacturer used two or more of these elements in his reaper, McCormick could take him to court and claim that he had copied his machine.

Ironically, it was three firms that McCormick hired to manufacture his reapers who fought hardest against his receiving an extension on his original patent. Seymour & Morgan; Backus, Fitch & Company; and J. Ganson & Company, all of Brockport, N.Y., wanted McCormick defeated in court. If McCormick's patent was not renewed, these companies would no longer have to pay McCormick a thirty dollar patent fee for each reaper they made. Obed Hussey joined them in the fight against McCormick's patent renewal.

Hussey presented a particular problem for McCormick, because he had been granted a patent on his reaper in 1833, while McCormick did not receive a patent until 1834. However, McCormick had actually built his first reaper in 1831. McCormick knew that many people would oppose him in his efforts for extension, and as early as 1846, he began to plan for the upcoming court battle. He especially needed people to testify that they had seen his reaper in 1831.

On October 13, 1846, McCormick wrote a letter to his brother William in Walnut Grove, asking about a neighbor, John McCown, who had made the sickle for McCormick's first reaper. His testimony would be invaluable.

McCormick also planned to rely on the testimonies of his mother, two brothers, John and Eliza Steele, and N.M. Hitt, all of whom witnessed the first field trial in 1831. He obtained signed statements from all of them, attesting that they witnessed McCormick's first reaper harvest wheat.

On December 10, 1847, a full six months before his patent was due to expire, McCormick applied to the U.S. Patent Office for an extension. He paid the required forty dollars, and his hearing was set for February 12, 1848. He was to appear before the Board of Patents, which consisted of U.S. Secretary of State James Buchanan; the commissioner of patents, Edmund Burke; and the solicitor of the treasury, Mr. Gillette. He began to prepare a long report, in which he told the story of his invention and how much it had benefitted the farmers. He wrote that, time and again, he had won field trials against Hussey, who was, he said, his only rival of any importance. McCormick also contended that the money he earned from the reaper was far less than the money that farmers saved by using it.

McCormick, however, made two mistakes. First, it did not occur to him that his own manufacturers would oppose his patent renewal. Rather, he assumed that Obed Hussey would be his primary opponent. Hussey's own patent was due to expire a few months before McCormick's. When Hussey failed to file with the Patent Office in time to renew his patent, McCormick's confidence soared. He wrongly assumed that he would now have no problem renewing his patent, as Hussey would now have to go through Congress to renew his, which was a much longer process.

Secondly, McCormick refused to hire an attorney to represent him in court. He thought that his expertise would enable him to best represent himself. McCormick presumed that the signed statements he had obtained from his witnesses were all that he needed to convince the Patent Board that he had invented a mechanical reaper before Hussey. He did not realize that those who opposed the renewal of his patent would, according to law, be able to question McCormick's witnesses in a formal hearing, called a deposition. If he had hired an attorney, the attorney would have informed McCormick of the deposition.

On February 1, 1848, McCormick found out about the deposition. He went to Baltimore to talk to Hussey, where he forced Hussey to admit that he had not invented his reaper until 1833. He was unable, however, to get Hussey to tell him when he planned to speak to his witnesses. This greatly irritated McCormick. On February 21, he spoke with Commissioner Burke and urged him to settle on a date for the deposition. He was eager to prove that he had invented his reaper before Hussey.

On February 21, the same day McCormick spoke to Commissioner Burke, Hussey wrote to the commissioner and objected to McCormick's patent renewal, saying that his rival's reaper "has not proved a useful invention to the public," and that giving McCormick a patent extension would hurt the man who had made "the best Reaping Machine which was ever offered to the world"—meaning himself. Hussey also wrote that McCormick had an unfair advantage in the Hutchinson field trial of 1843, because Hussey was not able to rescue his reaper from the island in the James River. He also said that McCormick's machine was of very poor quality. Hussey's claims were brazen. It was common knowledge that he was selling less than one hundred machines per harvest season, and McCormick, by this time, was selling over one thousand.

Hussey was also afraid that McCormick would easily prove he had invented his reaper first. On February 23, Hussey wrote another letter to the Board of Extension: "Our machines are different in principle, so far as regards these points, which either of us can justly claim to be the inventor of. I will admit that our machines in some respects are similar but these points of similarity are public property, and not the invention of either of us."

The Board of Extensions met on February 23 and decided to postpone a decision on McCormick's patent renewal until March 29, 1848. They instructed McCormick that, before March 29, he was to give the Board "satisfactory testimony that the invention of his machine was prior to the invention of a similar machine by Obed Hussey." They further instructed McCormick that he could determine the time and date that the depositions of the witnesses were to be taken.

On February 28, McCormick told Hussey that the depositions would be taken at Walnut Grove on March 17, and that he could attend if he wanted. On March 12, McCormick was in Charlottesville, Virginia, very ill with a fever. He wrote to William that he doubted he would be well enough to come to Walnut Grove by March 17. He further wrote: "I don't think that Hussey will attend to it at all . . . Mrs. Steele will not be there, and it will be important to have the case as strong as it can be . . . Mr. McCown stated that I called on him in 1831 to get a sickle made, which he did make . . . which he heard was put to such a machine that year but did not see . . . McCown must be got . . . See McCown as soon as possible and spare no pains to get all done right."

McCormick was wrong to believe that Hussey and Eliza Steele would not show up for the depositions on

March 17. Mrs. Steele had seen the first public trial of the reaper at Steele's Tavern in 1831. A few months before the depositions, she described it in writing for McCormick. However, in the months that followed, the aging Mrs. Steele became mentally unstable and could not remember anything that she had written to McCormick. Fearing that her failing memory would damage his case, McCormick prepared a paper for Mrs. Steele to read at the deposition. Of course, this made her testimony useless, since she was reading McCormick's words, not her own.

The Patent Board reconvened on March 29, 1848, to make a final decision. The commissioner of patents, Edmund Burke, said that McCormick deserved to have his patent renewed because of the "originality and priority" of his invention, the inadequacy of the compensation he received, and the reaper's importance to agriculture. Secretary of State Buchanan and Solicitor of the Treasury Gillett decided against McCormick's application. Burke was outvoted, two to one.

McCormick took every defeat personally, but this stung bitterly. He believed it was easier to fight a flesh and blood enemy rather than a principle, and so he decided to take Hussey on again. He appealed to Congress for the next ten years to renew his patent, but lost each time.

McCormick lost the fight over the patent, but it did little to deter his success. Despite the fact that others were now able to manufacture and sell reapers patterned after his, McCormick sold far more reapers than anyone in the country. He continued to aggressively market and improve the McCormick reaper. By 1848, he had became a millionaire—one of the few in the United States. His brother William wrote to him in February of 1859: "Your money has been made not out of your patents but by making and selling the machines . . . Others have been making all they could sell. You will not be able to collect patent fees is I suppose about the only difference it will make."

By contrast, as hard as Obed Hussey reportedly worked, his business at Baltimore did not grow. Even so, he declared, "I alone have been successful with a reaper in the United States and now believe myself without a rival in any country." Despite his boasting, Hussey's business continued for years to lag far behind McCormick's.

Losing the patent fight had many effects on McCormick's business. Although he was a millionaire, he now had to focus on building better reapers more efficiently and to market them even more aggressively. He could no longer depend on the patent fees for income, and he had to protect his business from unfair competition.

McCormick began to develop what he called "the finger ends of the business"—finding ways to expand sales and increase profits. He developed new methods, combined previous ideas into new arrangements, and expanded on earlier innovations. In the process, he made changes that remain part of business today.

McCormick began offering a written guarantee with every machine he sold that "warranted the performance of the Reaper in every respect." He had his guarantee printed like an advertisement, with a picture of the reaper at the top, and blank spaces for the farmer, the agent, and two witnesses to sign.

The guarantee came with a free trial period, one of the first times this device had ever been used. The price of the reaper was $120, with thirty dollars due at the signing of the guarantee, and the remaining ninety dollars due in six months. He promised the reaper would cut one and one half acres per hour, scatter less grain than the grain cradle, and enable the grain to be raked off from a raker's seat. If the reaper failed to perform any of these functions, the farmer could return the machine and McCormick would refund his thirty dollars.

McCormick also set non-negotiable prices for his reapers. Previously, many farmers had depended on a barter system, where items were traded and prices were haggled over. Set prices meant that no one got a "special deal," because all farmers paid the same amount. He knew this would inspire trust and take "pricing power" out of the hands of his salesmen, who would always be tempted to lower the price and make special arrangements in order to make a sale.

It soon became clear that McCormick was not a man to wait for his business to grow; he made it grow. He put the customer's needs first, which gained him the good will of the farmers. Although he did not purposely seek the admiration of others, he became widely admired and respected. He gave credit to qualified farmers so they could pay for their new reapers with money they saved from the harvest. He said, "It is better that I should wait for the money than that you should wait for the machine that you need." He lost some money this way, but the trust he earned was worth more than an occasional loss.

After McCormick developed the finger ends of the business, his sales quadrupled. The McCormick Reaper Factory was said to be the biggest manufacturing plant in the city of Chicago. The factory was a brick building, partly two stories and partly three stories high, measuring 40 by 190 feet. It housed three planing machines, six saws, two wood lathes, seven iron lathes, three boring machines, and a fan for blowing the fires of sixteen blacksmiths. The powerful engine that drove all the machinery was the wonder of the Chicago industrial community. The factory contained woodworking and ironworking departments, and by 1850, employed 120 men. Not only did McCormick own the factory, he also owned a long section of river frontage and a dock. He could therefore receive raw materials of wood, coal, and iron without having to pay high transfer charges across the city.

Chapter Six

The Crystal Palace

McCormick seized upon another opportunity in 1849, as thousands of men rapidly headed to California for the Gold Rush. He prepared an elaborate advertisement, pointing out to farmers that there would soon be a scarcity of farm labor. Laborers who were left, McCormick warned, would be in such high demand that they would insist on higher wages. He predicted that the grain crops of 1849 would be huge and would spoil in the fields, unless farmers bought his reaper. He concluded his ad with the exuberant testimonials of ninety-two farmers who had purchased his reaper.

McCormick assigned responsible agents at locations where the reapers were sold. He put a warehouse at each location so the farmers could buy a reaper and take it home the same day. One of McCormick's competitors complained that he "flooded the country with his machines." But McCormick knew that some farmers would be undecided about purchasing a reaper until the last minute before harvest, when it would be too late to ship one from Chicago. He soon had nineteen such agencies around the country.

Back in Chicago, disaster struck during the noon hour on March 25, 1851, when a fire broke out in the paint shop. A high wind spread the fire quickly, and the entire south wing of the factory was destroyed. Although the engine room at the center of the factory was fire-proof, overall damages exceeded seven thousand dollars, which was not covered by insurance. Worst of all, the fire had occurred in the midst of the spring manufacturing rush.

McCormick began reconstruction immediately, and by harvest time, he had completed all the reapers he had planned to build that year. The new, larger wing of the factory was even better than before. Great cisterns of water were placed underground in the factory yard and watchmen were employed around the clock. McCormick installed a new force pump with enough hose to reach the tin roofs of any building. All windows had fire-proof shutters. McCormick's factory was said to be the largest of its kind in the world, and the *Chicago Daily Journal* wrote on December 23, 1851, that McCormick "conquers nature to the benign end of civilization and brings bread to the mouths of the poor."

The McCormick factory was building and marketing fifteen hundred reapers to farmers from New York to

California, from Texas to New Jersey. The reaper had clearly proved its worth in America, and McCormick began to look abroad to Europe. Because of massive European immigration to the newly discovered gold fields in California and Australia, there was a labor shortage on the farms they left behind. In Ireland, many families had starved to death in a famine—laborers who had customarily migrated to England each season to harvest wheat. While the American farm laborer could harvest two acres per day with the cradle-scythe, the Irish laborer, using only a sickle, was lucky to harvest less than an acre of the heavy English wheat from sunrise to sunset.

In 1851, London, England, hosted the first world's fair, the Exhibition of the Industries of All Nations, and was building the Crystal Palace, an impressive hall made of iron and over a million feet of glass, to house the exhibition. McCormick saw the exhibition as a golden opportunity to introduce his reaper to Europe. He was accustomed to taking his reaper to farmers to demonstrate it, but at the Crystal Palace, his audience would come to him. He secured an English patent on his machine and sent a reaper to Europe, along with an expert mechanic named D.C. McKenzie from New York.

McCormick was not the only one to send a reaper to London—Hussey did as well. The third reaper to be exhibited was known as the Tollemache machine, named for a British member of Parliament, Thomas Tollemache, who had visited America in 1849. On his trip, he had seen a Hussey reaper at work and was so impressed by it that he talked his friend John Ellis into buying one, which he shipped to England from New York in June 1850.

An English manufacturing firm, R. Garrett & Son of Leiston, heard of Ellis's latest acquisition and paid him ten pounds for the privilege of copying Hussey's reaper. By 1851, the firm had produced two reapers of its own, and one was exhibited at the Crystal Palace. Hussey viewed this as an act of piracy and was outraged.

The Exhibition opened May 1, 1851. At first, English newspapers were very unkind to the American exhibitors. Anticipating more exhibitors than actually came, the United States commissioners had reserved far too much floor space in the Crystal Palace, and much of it stood conspicuously empty. Moreover, whereas the European exhibitors displayed beautiful works of art—silks, paintings, and statues—the American exhibitors brought everyday, practical items and inventions such as cotton cloth, nautical instruments, India-rubber shoes, a life boat, artificial arms and eyes, gold-filled teeth, air-exhausted coffins, sewing machines, maple sugar, slate pencils, cod-liver oil, corn-husk mattresses, railroad switches, and telegraph instruments. One exhibitor from Ohio displayed a "stuffed, buck-eyed squirrel."

As for McCormick's Virginia Reaper, the *London Times* called it "a cross between a flying machine, a wheelbarrow and an Astley chariot." Other newspapers called it "an extravagant Yankee contrivance," and described it as "huge, unwieldy, unsightly and incomprehensible." One reporter wrote: "Other nations rely upon their proficiency in the arts, or in manufactures, or in machinery, for producing effect. Not so with America. She is proud of her agricultural implements which [other countries] reject as worthless; she is proud of her machinery, which would hardly fill one corner of our Exhibition."

Though Europe scorned the American exhibitors, their opinion changed as the months went on. The Colt revolver, brought by Samuel Colt of Connecticut, proved better than all European firearms. The yacht *America* was faster than all other competitors. India-rubber, brought by Charles Goodyear of Connecticut, proved its usefulness in durable, waterproof goods. Day & Newell's Parautoptic Permutating Lock mystified all English locksmiths.

The crowning glory of the Americans was the Virginia Reaper, which went from being scorned in the *London Times* to being praised in the same newspaper as justifying the entire cost of the Exhibition, which had been attacked in some quarters as an extravagance pushed by Queen Victoria's German-born husband, Prince Albert.

The United States entered a total of 499 exhibits. Of these, five won Council Medals, 102 won Prize Medals, and fifty-three were awarded honorable mention. In proportion to the number of entries, America won more awards than the English exhibitors. The Council Medal was especially coveted by exhibitors, as it was "almost exclusively reserved as a reward for remarkable inventions, and was considered not to be applicable in cases where excellence of execution, however great, was the only merit."

McCormick's Virginia Reaper was one of the winners of the Council Medal. This honor was not given because the machine looked impressive sitting on the floor of the Crystal Palace. It cinched the medal because of its demonstration in the English fields.

Though the reaper had been in England since May 1, McCormick did not arrive in London until August 4. Earlier, B.P. Johnson, secretary of the New York State Agricultural Society and a judge at the Exhibition, suggested that the three reapers on exhibit—McCormick's, Hussey's, and Tollemache's—engage in a field trial. J.J. Mechi, a wealthy cutlery manufacturer in London, suggested that the reapers be tested on his farm at Tiptree Heath, forty-five miles away.

The trial was held on July 24, 1851. Neither Hussey nor McCormick was present, but two hundred people stood in the pouring rain to see their reapers compete in the green, wet wheat. Hussey's reaper was operated by an English mechanic who had been in charge of the reaper for the three months it had been at the Exhibition. However, he had never seen the reaper work. D.C. McKenzie operated McCormick's.

The Tollemache machine would not start and was disqualified from the contest. Hussey's mechanic started his machine, but the knife clogged and the raking-off process failed because the platform was not properly adjusted. Skeptics in the crowd cheered, for they believed that their misgivings about the reapers were about to be proven true.

Then McKenzie started the Virginia Reaper. The crowd watched as he moved it easily through the wheat. The judges estimated that the reaper moved at a speed that would enable it to harvest twenty acres a day. The crowd was impressed, but a Belgian judge skeptically suggested that they not proclaim the McCormick machine the winner until they could prove that it would harvest dry grain as well.

English newspapers published long articles about the McCormick reaper, and it became the most popular exhibit at the Crystal Palace. McKenzie was anxious for McCormick to come to England to witness the success. On July 29, 1851, he wrote in a letter to a friend, "Mr. McCormick has not yet arrived, and I look for him with great anxiety, as it is highly necessary he should be here."

McCormick arrived by boat on August 4. (Prone to seasickness, he was delighted to have just completed the first voyage in which he did not fall ill.) The next field trial had been set for two days later. Hussey was in France and would not attend. The trial was held on the farm of Philip Pusey, the chairman of the Committee on Agricultural Implements. McCormick was there, and his reaper performed flawlessly. Hussey's once again failed to operate well.

The judges were now satisfied that McCormick's reaper was superior to the others. *The London Times* reported that "the reaping machine from the United States is the most valuable contribution from abroad, to the stock of our previous knowledge, that we have yet discovered."

Hussey was outraged that McCormick's reaper had been declared the winner. He redoubled his efforts to market his machine in England. Once again, the McCormick and Hussey reapers met on the field, on September 25, 1851. McCormick had by this time returned to America. During the contest, McCormick's reaper failed to start, and Hussey's proved superior. Mechi ordered a Hussey reaper for his own harvest, and Hussey eventually had the honor of demonstrating his machine for Prince Albert of England, who immediately ordered two Hussey machines for the royal estates at Windsor and Osborne.

Many more Hussey/McCormick field trials took place in England in the ensuing years. At one point, Hussey's machine was favored, but then McCormick's gained popularity once again. Regardless of whose machine was better, English agriculture had forever changed. More grain was grown, and the reaper helped solve the hunger problem in Europe and raised standards of living.

McCormick fought furiously when he had been done an injustice. This was a family trait. The McCormick family motto was *Sine Timore*, or "Without Fear." One of McCormick's admirers later wrote: "He had certain clear, definite convictions, logical and consistent. What he knew—he knew. There were no hazy imaginings in his mind." An attorney who once worked for McCormick said: "[T]he exhibition of his powerful will was at times actually terrible. If any other man on this earth ever had such a will, certainly I have not heard of it."

It was this strong will and determination to prove himself right that caused McCormick to file one lawsuit after another throughout his career. Often he had several lawsuits in court at the same time, and many on appeal. He sued nearly every reaper manufacturer in the country, including some who had previously manufactured his own reapers. He even threatened to sue farmers who bought his rivals' reapers.

One of his most bitter lawsuits was filed against John H. Manny, who lived with his father, Pells Manny, in Waddam's Grove, Illinois. The Mannys became interested in manufacturing farm machinery and by 1850 had built a combined reaper and mower that met the enthusiastic approval of many farmers in the area. Although it looked like a McCormick reaper, it was different in many respects. McCormick, characteristically, was convinced that it infringed on his 1845 and 1847 patents.

After McCormick returned from England, he and John Manny clashed at the New York State Agricultural Society in the summer of 1852. Manny received first prize for his reaper and second prize for his mower. McCormick did not win any prizes. The *Albany Cultivator* proclaimed that Manny's machine was the best mower-reaper available. McCormick published a letter in which he listed the reasons why his machine, and not Manny's, should have won all the prizes.

The next year, a field trial was held in New Jersey. This time McCormick's machine was declared to be the best reaper-mower, but Manny again took first prize for the best reaper. McCormick began advertising in newspapers and farmers' magazines that Manny's machine was a copy of his.

On November 22, 1854, a McCormick agent, James Campbell, traveled to Rockford, Illinois, where Manny had set up a factory the previous year. Campbell purchased a Manny reaper, which he immediately sent to the McCormick factory. McCormick studied it very carefully, and a week later filed a lawsuit in the United States Circuit Court against Manny for patent infringement. In the lawsuit, McCormick said that Manny had made a great deal of money on the reaper, and had thus robbed McCormick of about thirty thousand dollars. McCormick asked the court to issue an injunction against Manny from manufacturing any more reapers from that point on. He also requested that Manny be forced to furnish McCormick with an accounting of his profits. The judge agreed to both requests.

Eleven months passed before the trial. McCormick had learned from his failure in the earlier patent case that he needed excellent legal counsel. He hired two lawyers: Edward N. Dickerson, a patent attorney, and Reverdy Johnson. Manny hired George Harding, a patent attorney from Philadelphia, and Peter H. Watson, a famous lawyer from Washington who had an astounding knowledge of harvesting machinery and patent law. He also hired prominent attorney Edwin M. Stanton, who would later serve as secretary of war during the Lincoln Administration.

Because the case was to be heard in Springfield, Illinois, the capital city, Manny's legal team decided that a local lawyer, who knew presiding Judge Drummond, would be advantageous for their defense. They hired a young lawyer named Abraham Lincoln. This was Lincoln's first big case, and it lasted for fourteen months. When a verdict was reached on January 16, 1856, it favored Manny in every respect.

McCormick, bitter at the defeat, immediately filed an appeal. Manny died on January 30, 1856, just days after he won the first case, but his heirs continued to fight the lawsuit that dragged on for two and one half years, until May 1858, when the United States Supreme Court again decided in favor of Manny.

Obed Hussey, seeking to take advantage of McCormick's defeats, decided to join the fray and filed a lawsuit against McCormick in 1858. Hussey claimed that McCormick had used an open-back guard finger with a vibrating scallop-edged cutter in his 1857 machine that were elements of his invention covered by his own 1847 patent. On September 19, 1859, the court ruled in favor of Hussey and ordered McCormick to stop using the finger and cutter in his reapers. McCormick was also ordered to pay Hussey $80,618.73 for patent infringement.

As America plummeted towards civil war at the end of the 1850s, the country came to value the reaper for political reasons. The primary cash crop of the South was cotton, and of the North, wheat. By 1861, there were as many reapers in the wheat fields of the North as could do the work of a million slaves. Many thought that the reaper even helped the North win the Civil War by taking the place of men in the fields, thus freeing them up to do battle with the South. Edwin M. Stanton, who had become the secretary of war during the Civil War, said: "The Reaper is to the North what Slavery is to the South. By taking the place of regiments of young men in the . . . harvest fields, it releases them to do battle for the Union at the front and at the same time keeps up the supply of bread for the Nation and the Nation's armies. Thus without McCormick's invention, I fear the North could not win and the Union would be dismembered."

Whether McCormick was conflicted over the outcome of the Civil War is not known. His original home was in the South, but he had settled in the North by the time the Civil War broke out. His own slaves had refused to leave Virginia and move to Illinois, and they could not be freed under Virginia state law until after Lincoln issued the Emancipation Proclamation. McCormick had abided by their wishes and rented them out to former neighbors near Walnut Grove. Also, his strong allegiance with the Democratic Party meant he was opposed to Republican President Abraham Lincoln.

What is clear is that by the middle of the nineteenth century, McCormick was a giant in the business world who had contributed enormously to the welfare of millions of people on two continents. Even so, he was not admired by everyone. Many regarded McCormick with fear because he was so powerful. He was often rude and considered a bully by some. He was impatient with those he considered small-minded, or whom he felt obstructed his path to success. He met obstacles— whether they were people or circumstances—with a determination to defeat them.

Chapter Seven

Marriage and Family

Over the years that he built his business, many changes had taken place within the McCormick family. With the new factory in Chicago, the Walnut Grove reaper operation had been permanently shut down, despite McCormick's occasional letters to his brothers suggesting that the family ought to maintain the old home. McCormick's mother, Polly, and sister Amanda Adams were the only members of the McCormick family left in the Valley of Virginia. On June 1, 1853, Polly died of typhoid fever in Amanda's home. By the end of the 1850s, Amanda and her husband Hugh had also moved to Chicago. Leander and William had both married and were living in Chicago and working in the reaper factory. Their sister Mary Caroline wed the Reverend James Shields on May 11, 1847, and had moved to Mexico, Pennsylvania.

In 1858, at the age of forty-nine, Cyrus McCormick

was the only one of his siblings who was still unmarried. The years McCormick spent devoted to his reaper manufacturing and marketing business had left him little time for a social life. His disposition and personality probably also contributed to his being alone. Even in his youth, "because of his sedateness he was never very popular with the girls, indeed he made no effort whatever to become so." However, years later his former slave Joe Anderson spoke of McCormick as a youth, saying, "sometimes he and I used to go out of an evening to see our girls, but we was always home again early at night, for late hours was against the rules of the house." At twenty-two, Cyrus had written to his cousin Adam McChesney, "Mr. Hart has two fine daughters, rite [sic] pretty, very smart, and as rich probably as you could wish; but alas! I have other business to attend to and can . . . devote but a small proportion of my time to the enjoyment of their society or any others."

McCormick's long bachelor status, evidently, was not due to lack of attention from women. Thomas J. Paterson wrote to William McCormick on February 18, 1855, "the last time I saw him [Cyrus McCormick] at Washington the Women were in full cry after him. He thought the *Dear Angels* wanted his money and ran the other way as fast as they pursued."

While McCormick traveled to Europe and various parts of the United States, marketing his reaper during the 1850s, he wrote many letters to his brothers William and Leander, who were in Chicago running the factory. Most often his letters were business-like, direct and to the point, with no hint of frivolity. His excellent health enabled him to do the work of two days in just one. He preached the merits of relaxation and exercise to his brothers, but never had time to take his own advice. He worked hard and expected others to do the same. In 1857, he wrote to William: "It will be necessary for you and L.J. [Leander] to *take care* to *avoid interruptions* from attention of body and mind to business, as much as possible . . . The business is entirely too large and the responsibilities *now* too immense to admit of a departure from *regular business system* and *hours* (of course some *exceptions*). This success in business is the foundation of *everything* . . . I don't want to be severe but you will know the importance of all I say, and *you* could *not fail* to feel it in my position."

Just four months later, though, McCormick wrote again: "And then, of course, first of all things, as I have always said, your place is to arrange to take as much time and exercise for yourself as your health requires to recruit it properly. This I have always urged upon you, and you can only judge of. While, as I said, I write and talk entirely about business, as necessary for so large a concern, I am sure I do feel constantly for the interests of you all, as a father does, being the oldest, and from the circumstances of my position in business, at the head, in a business point of view."

In August 1857, McCormick was in Chicago and had been there for six weeks, the longest he had stayed in that city in two years. Later the same month, William and Leander wrote to their sister, Mary Carolyn, that they "wouldn't be surprised if C. H. picked up a wife."

On September 23, forty-eight-year-old McCormick, who by this time had returned to New York, wrote his brother that he was awaiting an "important document from Chicago—more anon—till then 'nuff said.' " It was unlike McCormick to write in such a lighthearted manner and to use slang, and it made William and Leander even more suspicious about what was going on with their older brother.

William and Leander were right to be curious. Cyrus McCormick had met Miss Nancy Fowler from New York, who was visiting Mr. and Mrs. Isaac L. Lyon in Chicago. McCormick first saw "Nettie," as she liked to be called, one Sunday as she sang in the choir of a Chicago Presbyterian church. Soon they began "keeping company." After McCormick left for New York, their romance continued by correspondence. On September 25, he wrote to William that he had recently proposed marriage to Nettie in a letter. He was very nervous after he mailed the letter, and wrote, "It is *gone*, and I *suppose* I'm in for it."

To McCormick's delight, Nettie accepted his proposal, and the couple set January 26, 1858, as their wedding date. McCormick was busy in Washington with

Forty-nine-year-old Cyrus McCormick and twenty-five-year-old Nettie Fowler married on January 26, 1858.

the Manny case, and hoped he could get back to Chicago in time for the wedding. On December 25, 1857, McCormick wrote to William: "I trust that, under Providence, in the anticipated change in my mode of living, I shall realize a blessing . . . It would afford me great pleasure if, in view particularly of the contemplated change . . . I could settle down with you all, that we might be . . . all together, as a united family, and I hope this may yet be the case ere long."

Forty-nine-year-old Cyrus McCormick and twenty-five-year-old Nettie Fowler were wed at noon on January 26, 1858, at the home of Isaac Lyons. Reverend Nathan L. Rice of the North Presbyterian Church performed the ceremony. The new Mrs. McCormick was a devout Presbyterian, and the couple carried a Bible with them on all their trips together. Nettie also had a keen sense for business, and McCormick came to rely on her judgment and wise advice. She showed an enthusiasm for the manufacturing business, which delighted and gratified McCormick. He seldom made a business decision without her approval.

As McCormick was enjoying his recent marriage, news about his old rival Obed Hussey reached him. While traveling on a train one day in 1860, Hussey stepped off at a stop to get a glass of water for a thirsty child. While attempting to reboard the train, it suddenly lurched ahead. Hussey lost his balance, fell between two of the moving train cars, and was crushed. At the time of his death, Obed Hussey's business was said to be worth five hundred dollars.

Cyrus was also affected by his wife's compassionate nature. Nettie loved to help the less fortunate, and she saw her husband's wealth not as a way to further her own desires, but as a way to help others. Because of her example, McCormick became much more patient and considerate. He wrote to a friend, "I am in favor of using means [money] while one lives, rather than leave all to be lost or squandered, as it *may be*, after death."

McCormick gave away about $550,000 during his lifetime. Of that amount, $445,000 was given to the Presbyterian Church and its interests. McCormick was instrumental in moving the ailing Presbyterian Theological Seminary from Albany, Indiana, to Chicago. It was later named the McCormick Theological Seminary. He gave forty-five thousand dollars to the Democratic Party, of which he was a staunch member. He also gave twenty-five thousand dollars to his sisters and several nieces and nephews, twenty-five thousand dollars to the YMCA, and ten thousand dollars to various literary, art, and music societies. After the Civil War, he donated large sums to soldiers' widows and orphans.

Under his wife's influence, McCormick also began to enjoy society more. Nettie was very skilled at social graces and introduced her husband to people who were interested in McCormick's opinion on matters other than business. He found that people respected him for things he had to say on subjects such as politics. He began to see that business was not the only aspect of life.

Cyrus's favorite brother, William, suffered poor health throughout his life, and he finally died in 1865. Upon William's death, McCormick was as grief-stricken as he had been when his father died. William had always been a peace-maker between Cyrus and Leander, who did not get along. During his last illness, William begged Cyrus and Leander to work together harmoniously and "forbear one another in love!" Ironically, William's death drove the two surviving brothers further apart. Disputes over William's estate and how his children should inherit it caused strife between them. The two brothers would never heal their relationship.

Cyrus and Nettie McCormick had seven children, two of whom died in infancy: Cyrus Hall Jr., born in 1859; Mary Virginia, born 1861; Robert Fowler, born 1863 and died 1865; Anita Eugenie, born 1866; Alice, born 1870 and died 1871; Harold Fowler, born 1872; and Stanley Robert, born 1874.

The McCormicks adored their children but were stern parents. Both Mr. and Mrs. McCormick disliked laziness, especially in their children. Mrs. McCormick urged her children to record how long it took them to dress and brush their teeth in the morning. They agreed that their children should be taught the meaning of duty and the value of money. Though the family was very wealthy,

Cyrus's brother and business partner, William McCormick, died in 1865.

the children were taught that along with privilege came responsibility and obligation. Mr. and Mrs. McCormick taught by their own example to be honest, devout, and to serve those less fortunate.

The McCormick family was usually overrun with pets: kittens, two squirrels named Zip and Zoe, a parrot, mocking birds, canaries, and many horses. Zip and Zoe ran freely about the house until one of them met an untimely end by falling into an open heat register. Their horses, which all the McCormick boys learned to ride, had distinctive names, such as Napoleon, Achilles, and Princeton.

Cyrus McCormick loved to play croquet with his children. He also taught them to play billiards, where he loved pitting his skill against theirs. He bought his first billiard table in December 1866.

McCormick also loved to eat, and too much food and not enough exercise eventually made his muscular physique become portly. He especially loved rare roast beef and cherry pie, and he drank several glasses of both milk and water with his meals. Breakfast always consisted of a bowl of hot corn-meal mush and cold milk.

McCormick often took his family with him when business called him away from home. As passionate and stubborn as McCormick was about his reaper, he was equally obstinate and headstrong about smaller matters. On a railroad trip from Washington, D.C. to Chicago in 1862, he and his wife, two children, a cousin, and two servants stopped for a few days in Philadelphia. When it came time to board the train to return to Chicago, McCormick presented the station clerk with nine trunks, which were loaded onto the train. The clerk then charged McCormick a fee of $8.70 for excess baggage. He refused to pay, saying that the baggage had been carried without a fee from Washington to Philadelphia. The clerk nevertheless insisted that McCormick pay. An enraged McCormick took his family off the train and demanded that his baggage be unloaded as well. His trunks were buried beneath other baggage, however, and it was impossible to retrieve them. He and his family returned to their Philadelphia hotel, and their trunks went on towards Chicago.

The next morning, McCormick called J. Edgar Thompson, the president of the Pennsylvania Central Railroad, and told him what had happened. Thompson telegraphed the Pittsburgh station and instructed the station master to unload McCormick's baggage there. However, the order was not obeyed, and the nine trunks went all the way to Chicago, where they were placed in the unclaimed baggage area. That night, lightning struck the station and burned it to the ground. Four of the nine trunks were saved, but five were completely destroyed. Nettie prepared a list of their burned possessions, which included diamonds and other jewelry given to her by her husband shortly before their marriage. The lost property was valued at fifty-five hundred dollars. McCormick decided to sue the railroad, charging that it had stolen their trunks after refusing to unload them at the Philadelphia station as McCormick had demanded.

McCormick's lawsuit against the railroad dragged on in the courts for years. McCormick won the initial case, but the railroad appealed. McCormick won again, and the railroad again appealed. The case went all the way to the Supreme Court. Eighteen years later, McCormick finally won and was awarded over eighteen thousand dollars—but he did not live to see it. Legal fees exceeded his winnings, but had McCormick lived, he would have been pleased that he was at last proven right.

In spite of McCormick's deep affection for his family, he maintained an intense work schedule. He was often up at dawn and at his desk answering correspondence or thinking about ways to improve his business. He took a brisk walk after breakfast then went to his office. Back home he often could be found at his desk until midnight. Late in his life he wrote, "If I had given up business, I would have been dead long ago."

Chapter Eight

Work to the End

Chicago had grown quickly and somewhat carelessly with the coming of the railroad. There were more than eleven hundred factories, of which McCormick's remained the largest and best known. Many of the factories turned out wood products, and endless stacks of lumber lined the Chicago River. Wood was used almost exclusively for building Chicago's tens of thousands of homes, businesses, and bridges. Even fifty-seven miles of streets and 561 miles of sidewalks were paved with wood.

The summer of 1871 had been unusually dry. By early October, Chicago had received only an inch and a half of rain since Independence Day. Around 9:00 P.M. on Sunday, October 8, a fire started in a two-story wooden cow barn behind Patrick O'Leary's cottage at 137 DeKoven Street on Chicago's west side. Firemen quickly responded to the first alarm, but a strong southwest wind accelerated the flames, and by 1:30 A.M. on October 9, the fire had jumped the river, engulfed the business district, and raced northward.

Firemen did their best to contain the fire, but to no avail. Preceding the wall of flames were showers of hot firebrands (small pieces of burning material), blown by the gale force wind. The firebrands fell on wooden roofs, broke through windows in homes and businesses, and fell onto lawns. Each fallen firebrand started a new fire. Homes, businesses, bridges, streets, and sidewalks burned out of control. The people of Chicago panicked as flames roared wildly, leaping rapidly from block to block. Nothing seemed to slow the fire's progress.

Rain began to fall at midnight on October 9—twenty-seven hours after the fire had started—and helped put out the fire. When the last of the flames had died out, twenty-six hundred acres of the city had burned—a strip about four miles long and three quarters of a mile wide. Three hundred people were dead and one hundred thousand were homeless. Eighteen thousand buildings worth a total of two hundred million dollars lay in ashes.

McCormick's reaper factory and two thousand reapers were lost in the fire. His wife and children were in New York, and McCormick sent Nettie a telegram asking her to come to Chicago at once. Leaving the children in the care of servants, she boarded a train and arrived in Chicago on October 11. McCormick met his

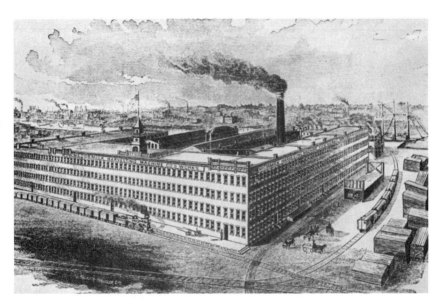

McCormick built a larger factory after the first one was damaged in the Chicago Fire of 1871.

wife at the train station wearing a half-burned coat and hat.

McCormick and Nettie had a decision to make. He was sixty-two years old and a multi-millionaire. Should they rebuild the factory, or should Cyrus retire? Nettie's immediate answer matched his: They would rebuild.

A temporary factory was erected on the site of the old one, and reapers for the next harvest season were soon in production. McCormick and his brother Leander decided that the new factory should be built at a different site, and work began in August 1872. The new factory was much larger and finer than the old one and was producing reapers by January 1873. The relationship between Cyrus and Leander was still strained, however, made worse when Leander further angered his brother by saying publicly that Cyrus did not invent the reaper, but that their father had.

An improvement was made to the McCormick reaper in 1873, after the company bought the patents for a harvester attachment from Charles and William Marsh. The harvester carried the grain from the platform to a bin, where it could be more easily bound by a farmer riding on the machine itself. Before, three or four binders would walk behind the reaper to bind the wheat, a job that could now be accomplished by one worker. The new innovation made McCormick's reaper much more efficient.

By 1875, when McCormick reached the age of sixty-six, rheumatism made it difficult for him to walk. Morning and evening, his arms and legs were massaged to relieve the stiffness and pain. His doctor expressed concern about his diet, and urged him to cut back on meat, fish and coffee, but McCormick did not follow his advice.

Despite his aging, McCormick worked to give his family the best life he could. For years, he and his wife had planned to build a mansion on Rush Street, where they owned a large lot. They broke ground for the home in 1876, and in 1879, it was completed. They were pleased to read in the *Chicago Daily Tribune*: "[The McCormick home is] the chief of the many private

The McCormicks built a fine home on 675 Rush Street.

residences which have made Chicago noted as a city where not only solidity and wealth but genuine taste in art prevails."

In the summer of 1878, McCormick went to Europe for the Paris Exposition, keeping himself as busy as ever. He received honors for his reaper, and on October 20, was promoted to officer of the Legion of Honor by the French minister of agriculture. The next day, McCormick was honored at the Palace of Industry in a gala affair, where he received medals for his achievements.

That night he felt tired and decided to go to bed early. He gratefully removed his collar where a sore spot on the back of his neck made it painful to wear. By morning, the sore spot had become a painful pimple. Specialists were brought in, and McCormick was diagnosed with a cancerous carbuncle. It needed to be punctured and drained, and McCormick, characteristically, refused anesthetic. Following this procedure, he became very ill, trembling with a high fever. By November 11, 1878, the crisis was over, but Nettie McCormick wrote to her son Cyrus Jr.: "He seemed shattered, as I never saw him before . . . [he] could not collect his mind readily . . . Papa is now certainly better . . . thank God his life is spared."

McCormick's body never completely recovered. He became an invalid, unable to walk without a cane or crutch. He was sometimes too feeble to leave his bed or wheel chair. He relied more and more upon his wife and eldest son to carry out or make business decisions. Often he showed no interest in business at all and dozed at the table during meals with his food untouched. As he grew older, his thoughts often turned to his boyhood in the Valley of Virginia. Tears would fill his eyes as he reminisced, and he once remarked to his valet, "Oh Charlie, how I wish I could get on a horse and ride through those mountains once again!"

In May 1880, the McCormicks gave a grand party in honor of Cyrus Jr.'s twenty-first birthday. Cyrus Jr. had graduated from Princeton in 1879, before joining his father and Uncle Leander in partnership at the newly renamed McCormick Harvesting Machine Company. Three hundred guests attended the flower-filled mansion to be entertained by an orchestra and various famous vocalists. After the concert, the guests took a tour of the home and were awestruck by the deep, lush carpets, beautiful woodwork, breathtaking frescoes on the ceilings, rich tapestries, and opulent furniture from all over the world. Mother Goose characters were painted on the walls of the nursery, and the tiles around the nursery fireplace depicted Bible stories.

For six more years, McCormick fought against old age. He traveled to New York mineral springs, in whose waters he felt his rheumatism was alleviated. He submitted to electrical treatments and prescription medications. Nevertheless, on April 30, 1884, he suddenly weakened. After improving four days later, he relapsed again on May 7. His doctors worked hard to save him, but old age had triumphed over Cyrus McCormick. Early in the morning on May 11, he gathered his family around him. He led them in prayer, and they sang several Presbyterian hymns.

The last words he spoke were, "Work, work!" before falling into unconsciousness. At 7:00 on the morning of May 13, 1884, seventy-five-year-old Cyrus McCormick died.

His funeral was held two days later. Much was said about McCormick at his passing, but the most expressive message was a wordless one: Standing by his casket was a gift from the workmen of his factory—a reaper made of flowers, with the main wheel missing. Across the reaper lay a sheaf of ripe wheat.

In 1879, Cyrus Jr. had joined McCormick Harvesting Machine Company, and following his father's death in 1884, he took over as president. Six years later, McCormick machines made up thirty-five percent of the farm equipment used on American farms. But the company was far from invulnerable. Many rivals threatened the McCormick Company's hold on the market, and Cyrus Jr. worried that they might succumb to the rigors of competition.

Banker J.P. Morgan offered Cyrus a solution that secured his company's future in American business. By merging with three of its larger competitors, the McCormick company grew into a giant that soon held eighty-five percent of the American farm machinery market. Morgan suggested calling the trust "International Harvester," a name which still represents the kind of quality farm equipment that Cyrus McCormick began making in 1831.

Sources

CHAPTER ONE: THE VALLEY OF VIRGINIA

p. 11, "My father was both . . ." William T. Hutchinson, *Cyrus Hall McCormick: Seed-Time, 1809–1856* (New York: The Century Company, 1930), 34.

p. 18, "You should carry a dictionary . . ." Herbert N. Casson, *Cyrus Hall McCormick: His Life and Work* (Chicago: A.C. McClurg & Co., 1909), 145.

p. 18, "That boy is beyond me." Ibid., 27.

CHAPTER TWO: BUILDING A DREAM

p. 22, "An insurmountable . . ." Casson, *Life and Work*, 43.

p. 25, "This machine is worth . . ." Ibid., 40.

CHAPTER THREE: WAR OF THE REAPERS

p. 28, "Perhaps I may make . . ." Casson, *Life and Work*, 53.

p. 28, "This thought was . . ." Ibid., 53-54.

p. 30, "sail about a little . . ." Craig Canine, *Dream Reaper* (New York: Knopf, 1995), 29.

p. 31, "Dear Sir: Having seen . . ." Ibid., 31-32.

p. 34, "the full and exclusive . . ." Hutchinson, *Seed-Time,* 93.

p. 34, "In 1836 . . ." Ibid., 128.

p. 37, "I consider myself alone . . ." Ibid., 32.

p. 39, "I am frank to say . . ." Ibid., 144.

p. 39, "intend[ed] to devote . . ." Robert Sobel, "Cyrus Hall McCormick: From Farm Boy to Tycoon" In *Writing About Business and Industry,* Beverly E. Schneller, Ed. (New York: Oxford University Press, 1995), 111.

p. 40, "It shall be . . ." Hutchinson, *Seed-Time*, 172-173.
p. 41, "I have thought it due . . ." Ibid., 190.
p. 41, "From the following . . ." Ibid.
p. 41, "give McCormick a go" Ibid., 191
p. 43, "This thing must end . . ." Ibid., 194.
p. 43, "degenerated into . . ." Ibid.

CHAPTER FOUR: EXPANSION
p. 46, "the machines are . . ." Cyrus McCormick, *The Century of the Reaper* (New York: Houghton Mifflin Co., 1931), 50.
p. 51, "It seems wrong . . ." McCormick, *Century*, 26.
p. 51, "I consider it . . ." Hutchinson, *Seed-Time*, 235.
p. 52, "will cut from . . ." Ibid.
p. 54, "You know well that . . ." Ibid., 239.

CHAPTER FIVE: CHICAGO
p. 56, "Many of the populous . . ." Hutchinson, *Seed-Time*, 255.
p. 58, "was born close to . . ." Casson, *Life and Work*, 76.
p. 60, "keep regular . . ." Hutchinson, *Seed-Time,* 260.
p. 61, "and monthly thereafter . . ." Ibid., 261.
p. 62, "untrue and false" Ibid., 263.
p. 66, "has not proved . . ." Ibid., 286.
p. 66, "the best Reaping Machine . . ." Ibid.
p. 66, "Our machines . . ." Hutchinson, *Seed-Time*, 269.
p. 67, "satisfactory testimony . . ." Ibid., 287.
p. 67, "I don't think that Hussey . . ." Ibid., 289
p. 68, "originality and priority" Ibid., 290.
p. 69, "I alone have been . . ." Canine, *Dream Reaper*, 37.
p. 70, "warranted the performance . . ." Ibid.

CHAPTER SIX: THE CRYSTAL PALACE
p. 71, "It is better . . ." Canine, *Dream Reaper*, 85.
p. 72, "flooded the country . . ." Ibid., 83.
p. 73, "conquers nature . . ." Hutchinson, *Seed-Time*, 271.
p. 75, "stuffed, black-eyed squirrel." Ibid., 386.
p. 76, "a cross between . . ." Ibid., 386.

p. 76, "an extravagant Yankee contrivance." Ibid.
p. 76, "huge, unwieldy . . ." Ibid.
p. 76, "Other nations rely upon . . ." Ibid., 396-397.
p. 77, "almost exclusively reserved . . ." Ibid., 388.
p. 78, "Mr. McCormick has not yet . . ." Ibid., 390.
p. 79, "the reaping machine . . ." Hutchinson, *Seed-Time*, 391.
p. 80, "He had certain clear . . ." Ibid., 151.
p. 83, "The Reaper is to . . ." Canine, *Dream Reaper*, 45.

CHAPTER SEVEN: MARRIAGE AND FAMILY
p. 86, "because of his sedateness . . ." Hutchinson, *Seed-Time*, 25.
p. 86, "sometimes he and I . . ." Ibid.
p. 86, "Mr. Hart has two fine daughters . . ." Ibid.
p. 86, "the last time I saw him . . ." Ibid., 457.
p. 87, "It will be necessary . . ." Ibid., 456.
p. 87, "And then, of course . . ." Ibid., 457.
p. 88, "wouldn't be surprised . . ." Ibid., 458.
p. 88, "important document . . ." Ibid.
p. 88, "It is gone, and I suppose . . ." Ibid., 459.
p. 90, "I trust that, under Providence . . ." Ibid.
p. 91, "I am in favor . . ." William T. Hutchinson, *Cyrus Hall McCormick: Harvest, 1856–1884* (New York: D. Appleton-Century Company, 1935), 5.
p. 92, "forbear one another . . ." Hutchinson, *Harvest,* 129.
p. 96, "If I had given up . . ." Casson, *Life and Work,*139.

CHAPTER EIGHT: WORK TO THE END
p. 100, "[The McCormick home is] . . ." Casson, *Life and Work* Ibid., 742.
p. 102, "He seemed shattered . . ." Hutchinson, *Harvest,* 673.
p. 102, "Oh Charlie . . ." George Iles. *Leading American Inventors* (New York: Books for Libraries Press, 1912), 314.
p. 103, "Work, work!" Casson, *Life and Work,* 187.

Bibliography

Bidwell, Percy Wells and John I. Falconer. *History of Agriculture in the Northern United States, 1620–1860*. Washington, D.C.: Carnegie Institution, 1925.

Bolton, Sarah Knowles. *Lives of Poor Boys Who Became Famous*. New York: Crowell, 1962.

Canine, Craig. *Dream Reaper*. New York: Knopf, 1995.

Casson, Herbert N.,*Cyrus Hall McCormick: His Life and Work*. Chicago: A.C. McClurg & Co., 1909.

Gates, Paul W. *Agriculture and the Civil War*. New York: Alfred A. Knopf, 1965.

Grun, Bernard. *The Timetables of History: A Horizontal Linkage of People and Events*. New York: Touch Stone, 1963.

Hutchinson, William T. *Cyrus Hall McCormick: Harvest, 1856–1884*. New York: D. Appleton-Century Company, 1935.

————*Cyrus Hall McCormick: Seed-Time, 1809–1856*. New York: The Century Company, 1930.

Iles, George. *Leading American Inventors*. New York: Books for Libraries Press, 1912.

Krooss, Herman E. and Charles Gilbert. *American Business History*. Englewood Cliffs, N.J.: Prentice-Hall Inc., 1972.

McCormick, Cyrus. *The Century of the Reaper*. New York: Houghton Mifflin Co., 1931.

Schultz, Gladys Denny. *Jenny Lind: The Swedish Nightingale.* Philadelphia: Lippencott, 1962.

Seligman, Ben B. *The Potentates: Business and Businessmen in American History.* New York: Dial Press, 1971.

Sobel, Robert. "Cyrus Hall McCormick: From Farm Boy to Tycoon" *Writing About Business and Industry,* Beverly E. Schneller, Ed. New York: Oxford University Press, 1995.

WEBSITES

Wisconsin Historical Society Archives: Cyrus Hall McCormick.
http://www.shsw.wisc.edu/archives/ihc/cyrus.html

Shenandoah Valley Agricultural Research and Extension Center: McCormick Farm.
http://www.vaes.vt.edu/steeles/mccormick/mccormick.html

Index